DISCO

C000134613

1 Find a time when you can read the Bible each day

2 Find a place where you can be quiet and think

4 Ask God to help you understand what you read

3 Grab your Bible and a pencil or pen

5 Read today's Discover page and Bible bit

6 Pray about what you have read and learned

We want to...

- Explain the Bible clearly to you
- Help you enjoy your Bible
- Encourage you to turn to Jesus
- Help Christians follow Jesus

Discover stands for...

- Total commitment to God's Word, the Bible
- Total commitment to getting its message over to you

Team Discover

Martin Cole, Nicole Carter, Rachel Jones, Kirsty McAllister, Alison Mitchell, André Parker, Ben Woodcraft Discover is published by The Good Book Company, Blenheim House, 1 Blenheim Rd, Epsom, Surrey, KT19 9AP, UK. thegoodbook.com | thegoodbook.co.uk | thegoodbook.com.au | thegoodbook.co.nz | thegoodbook.co.in ISBN: 9781784980566 | Printed in Turkey

How to use Discover

Here at Discover, we want you at home to get the most out of reading the Bible. It's how God speaks to us today. And He's got loads of top things to say.

We use the New International Version (NIV) of the Bible. You'll find that the NIV and New King James Version are best for doing the puzzles in Discover.

The Bible has 66 different books in it. So if the notes say…

Read Mark 14 v 1

…turn to the contents page of your Bible and look down the list of books to see what page Mark begins on. Turn to that page.

"Mark 14 v 1" means you need to go to chapter 14 of Mark, and then find verse 1 of chapter 14 (the verse numbers are the tiny ones). Then jump in and read it!

Here's some other stuff you might come across…

WEIRD WORDS

Sprongpip
These boxes explain baffling words or phrases we come across in the Bible.

Think!

This bit usually has a tricky personal question on what you've been reading about.

Action!

Challenges you to put what you've read into action.

Wow!

This section contains a gobsmacking fact that sums up what you've been reading about.

Pray!

Gives you ideas for prayer. Prayer is talking to God. Don't be embarrassed! You can pray in your head if you want to. God still hears you! Even if there isn't a Pray! symbol, it's a good idea to pray about what you've read anyway.

Coming up in Issue 4...

Mark: God's resue plan

First off we get stuck into the final few chapters of Mark's Gospel. We'll see how Jesus was let down by his friends and killed by his enemies. It's seriously shocking stuff — but none of it was a surprise to God. Jesus' death was all part of God's amazing rescue plan — a plan to rescue us too!

Ruth: The whole truth

Imagine leaving your home country, friends and family, to go to a totally new place where you have no food, no job, and no husband! Sound tough? That's exactly what Ruth did! But God was looking after Ruth and her mother-in-law Naomi, and showing them how loving and kind He is. In this issue of Discover we'll be reading their story in the little Bible book of Ruth. (Spoiler alert: it ends with a wedding!)

Genesis: Dreamer drama

We dive into Genesis to meet Joseph: a man who proves that dreams really do come true... at least, they do if you've got God working things out behind the scenes!

Joseph went from being his dad's fav son... to being locked up in jail... to being the second-most-important man in Egypt! Through Joe's good times and bad times, we learn that

God is totally in control, and working for the good of His people!

Acts: Spreading the word

Have you ever eaten a camel burger? Or a kangaroo steak? No? Well, Peter certainly hadn't! Until he received a strange vision from God...

It was all God's way of telling Peter and the other apostles that the good news about Jesus wasn't only for Jewish people — it's for **everyone**, no matter where they're from or what they eat!

Once the apostles got that, there was no stopping them — they set sail on some epic journeys around the world to tell lots of people about Jesus! Read all about it in Acts!

Colossians: Just Jesus

Finally, we get our heads into Colossians — a letter written by Paul to the Christians in Colossae, in Turkey.

False teachers had been telling the Colossians that they needed to do extra stuff to be right with God. Paul is writing to warn the Colossians: "DON'T LISTEN!" Paul reminds them how amazing Jesus is, and says that all they have to do is trust in Him. It's the same for us, too!

Ready to get started?
Then turn this page...

Mark: God's rescue plan

Mark
14 v 1-9

WEIRD WORDS

Passover and Festival of unleavened bread
We'll explain these tomorrow!

Chief priests and teachers of the law
Religious leaders who hated Jesus

Alabaster
White stone

Pure nard
A spiky plant

Indignantly
Angrily

Rebuked her
Told her off

The gospel
The great news that Jesus can rescue us

Welcome to issue 4 of Discover! Let's jump into Mark's book about Jesus. We join the amazing story of Jesus Christ, just a few days before His death.

Why did He die?

What amazing things happened? Let's find out...

Read Mark 14 v 1-2

The murder plan
Jesus' enemies hated Him and wanted to get rid of Him. They were trying to find a way to have Him killed.

Read verses 3-9

This woman poured a whole jar of expensive perfume over Jesus' head. She was showing how much she loved Him. Some people thought it was a waste of perfume and money (v4-5).

But Jesus said it was a beautiful thing, which is why we're reading about it 2000 years later (v9).

Think!
Do you love Jesus? How do you show your love for Him?

According to Jesus, why did Mary pour perfume on His body? (v8) Go back one letter (B=A, C=B, D=C etc) to find out.

U P   Q S F Q B S F

N F   G P S   N Z

C V S J B M

Jesus knew that He would soon die. Maybe His enemies' murder plan would work.

God's rescue plan!
Amazingly, it was always part of God's plan that Jesus would die. Not so that His enemies could get rid of Him, but so that Jesus could rescue His people.

Pray!
Thank God for His amazing rescue plan. Ask Him to help you show your love for Jesus by living to please Him.

Fest-of-all

Mark 14 v 12-16

Where's the busiest place you've ever been?

_____

_____

_____

_____

_____

_____

In Jerusalem, 2000 years ago, the busiest and most important time of the year was the Passover festival.

1000s of people travelled to Jerusalem, some from other countries. The city was crammed with people.

Each family had to buy a perfect lamb, kill it and offer it to God as a sacrifice. (You'll find out why tomorrow!)

Each family needed a room so that the lamb could be cooked and eaten.

Jesus wanted to eat His last ever Passover feast with His friends, the disciples. But in the overcrowded city, where could they possibly find a room where they could eat it together?

Read Mark 14 v 12-16

What did Jesus tell His disciples to look for? Cross out all the Xs, Zs and Ks, and follow the maze.

K	X	Z		K	Z	K
X	Z	K	A	Z	R	Z
Z	X	X	M	K	A	Z
X	C	N	A	X	J	R
K	A	K	K	X	Z	E
K	R	R	Y	K	A	T
Z	K	Z	I	Z	W	X
X	X	Z	N	G	A	K

__ ___ ___

___ ___ ___ ___ ___ __

___ ___ ___ ___ ___

The man led them to a large room, all set up for the feast! The disciples must have been amazed when everything turned out exactly as Jesus had said.

Jesus' enemies were plotting to kill Him. Yet Jesus was in total control of everything. It was all part of **God's rescue plan**.

Pray!

Thank God that He is in control of everything. If you mean it, tell God that you want Him to be in charge of your life.

Passover facts

**Exodus
12 v 3-14**

*Jesus was going
to celebrate
Passover with His
disciples.*

*But what was this
Passover thing all
about?*

WEIRD WORDS

Without defect
Perfect

Slaughter
Kill

In haste
Quickly!

Gods of Egypt
God would punish
the Egyptians for
worshipping fake
gods

Commemorate
Remember and
celebrate

Ordinance
Law

They were remembering a time
1500 years earlier, when God
rescued the Israelites from slavery
in Egypt.

To rescue His people, God sent
ten plagues on Egypt, but Pharaoh
wouldn't listen. Only after God killed
the eldest son (firstborn) of all the
Egyptians, did Pharaoh finally let the
Israelites go.

*Read the verses and fill in what the
Israelites had to do.*

Read Exodus 12 v 3-6

1. K_____ a l_____

The lamb was killed instead of the
firstborn son in each Israelite family.
The eldest son could say: *"That lamb
died instead of me!"*

Wow!

The lamb's death was a
picture of what JESUS would do
1500 years later.

He would die on the cross to take
the punishment we should get for
our sins. So Christians can look to
Jesus and say:

"He died instead of me!"

Read verses 8-11

2. E_____ the lamb

There were special instructions for
how the lamb should be cooked and
eaten. And the Israelites had to get
ready for their escape from Egypt!

Read verses 7 & 12-14

3. Use the lamb's bl_____

They had to put the lamb's blood on
their door frames. No blood would
mean death for the eldest son.

But if there was blood there,

God promised to p_____

o_____ the house and

not kill the eldest son (v13).

Pray!

If you're a Christian, thank God
for sending Jesus to die in your
place. Praise Him that on the day
of judgment, He will pass over
you and not punish you, because
of Jesus' death.

4

Traitor!

Judas

Jesus is eating His last ever Passover feast with His friends, the 12 disciples.

Well, 11 of them are His friends...

Read Mark 14 v 10-11

Judas had gone behind Jesus and the disciples' backs. He agreed to help Jesus' enemies with their plan to murder Jesus! What a traitor!

Now read Mark 14 v 17-21

When it was **evening**, Jesus and His twelve disciples came for the **Passover** meal. As they were **eating**, Jesus told His **disciples:** "One of you will **betray** me". This **upset** the disciples. "**Surely** you don't mean me!' they all said. **Jesus** answered: "It is one of you **twelve**, one who dips his **bread** in the bowl with me."

*Fit all the **bold** words into the grid. The shaded boxes should spell out two words.*

God's rescue plan!

Even before Jesus was born, the Old Testament said that God would send someone to rescue His people. That person was Jesus. But the Old Testament also said that He would have to suffer and die to rescue us (Isaiah 53 v 5). Amazingly, it was all part of God's rescue plan!

Judas did a terrible thing. He would be punished for it later. But Judas couldn't stop God's perfect plans. Nobody can! Instead, Judas himself became part of God's great rescue plan!

Pray!

Thank God that no one stops His perfect plans to rescue people.

Want to know more?
For the free e-booklet
Why Did Jesus Die?, email
discover@thegoodbook.co.uk
or check out
www.thegoodbook.co.uk/contact-us
to find our UK mailing address.

WEIRD WORDS

The Twelve
The 12 disciples. They were Jesus' friends and were taught by Him.

Reclining at the table
They lay on couches while eating a meal!

Son of Man
Jesus

Woe to...
God will punish that person

Amazing meal deal!

5

Mark
14 v 22-25

What's the most memorable meal you've eaten?

_____

_____

_____

Today we read about the most important meal... ever!

Only a few hours before His death, Jesus used this meal to show His friends what He was about to go through for them...

Read Mark 14 v 22

> When Jesus broke the bread and gave it to His disciples, He said:
>
> **"This is my _____"**
>
> So what did He mean?

The broken bread was a symbol of Jesus' body, which would be broken (tortured and killed) very soon.

Eating the bread showed the disciples that they would share in the good that came from Jesus' death for them.

Read verses 23-25

> What strange thing did Jesus say about the wine?
>
> **"This is my _____"**
>
> What did He mean now?

Blood gives life to our bodies. When Jesus died on the cross, He gave His life for others.

Drinking the wine reminded the disciples that Jesus would give His life for them, so their sins could be forgiven.

Blood of the covenant (v24)

A *covenant* is a promise. God promises to forgive people for the wrong things (sins) they've done. But only people who trust Jesus' death to rescue them from the punishment they deserve.

Christians still eat bread and drink wine together to remember that Jesus died for them. This meal is called the **Lord's Supper** or **Communion**.

Think & Pray!

What can you do to remind you that Jesus died for you?

_____

_____

_____

(Maybe you could make a poster of Romans 5 v 8.)

Now ask God to help you fully understand why Jesus suffered and died.

Stand and deliver

*It's night time
on the Mount of
Olives and danger
is approaching for
Jesus.*

*Will the disciples
face it with Jesus
or run away?*

WEIRD WORDS

Mount of Olives
Large hill

Galilee
Area where Jesus
grew up

Disown me
Pretend not to know
Jesus

**Insisted
emphatically**
Peter said that he'd
definitely not disown
Jesus

Read Mark 14 v 26-28

Jesus told His disciples that they'd all
leave Him when trouble came. Just
like sheep scattering when they're
scared! But Peter refused to believe
it...

Read verses 29-31

*How many times did Jesus say Peter
would deny knowing Him?*

Did Peter believe Jesus?

YES/NO _____

But Jesus knew that His friends
would all leave Him.

Standing up for Jesus can be really
hard. We don't want people to give
us a hard time for going to church
or believing in Jesus. So we find it
hard to own up to being a Christian.
Or we keep quiet when people say
things against Jesus.

Jesus had already told His followers
that they should expect to get
hassled for loving Him (it's in Mark
13 v 9-11).

But Jesus also told them that He'd
help them out in tricky situations.

*Use the **backwards** word pool to
complete Jesus' words from **Mark
13 v 11**.*

nevig   yloH   yas
tiripS   emit   tahw
yrrow   uoy

Do not w_____ about
w_____ to say. Just s_____
whatever is g_____ you
at the t_____. Because it
is not y_____ speaking, but
the H_____ S_____!

Wow!

When we're being hassled or
questioned about what we believe,
we should speak out!

Jesus has given all Christians His
Holy Spirit to help them tell people
about Him!

Pray!

Ask God to help you stand up
for Jesus. Ask Him to give you
the right words to say, and the
courage to say them.

**Mark
14 v 32-36**

WEIRD WORDS

Abba
Daddy

A	
B	
C	
D	
E	
F	
G	
H	
I	
L	
M	
N	
O	
R	
S	
T	
U	
W	
Y	

Garden of grief

Read Mark 14 v 32-34

Jesus prayed with three of His disciples in a quiet garden called

_ _ _ _ _ _ _ _ _ _ _ _ _ _

Why was Jesus upset?

Peter would let Him down ☐

Judas was on his way with a group of soldiers ☐

He knew He was going to die very soon ☐

All these reasons were bad enough, but there was something far worse that really hurt Jesus.

> Jesus knew that His Father would punish Him for the wrong things people have done. He didn't deserve to die, but it was the only way He could rescue us!

Read verses 35-36

No wonder Jesus fell to the ground in distress. No wonder He asked God to *"take this cup away from me"*.

He was asking God not to punish Him. He knew it would be like drinking from a cup full of God's punishment.

Use the code to reveal Jesus' amazing prayer.

_ _ _ _ _ _ _ _ _

_ _ _ _ _ _

_ _ _ _ _ _ _ _ _

_ _ _ _ _ _

Jesus wanted to obey His Father God even though that meant He would have to suffer and die!

Action!

In your prayers, make sure you ask what GOD wants, not just what YOU want.

Go on, try it right now...

Pray!

Obeying God is soooo hard. Ask Him to help you live for Him and please Him more.

Dozing disciples

Mark
14 v 37-42

Some people sleep through anything – alarm clocks, science lessons, church meetings.

Are you feeling sleepy?

Then WAKE UP!!

Jesus is in the garden of Gethsemane at night, praying to His Father God. Jesus is upset because He knows God will soon punish Him for people's sins.

Three disciples were with Jesus that night. Who were they (v33)?

P _ _ _ _

J _ _ _

J _ _ _ _

Jesus told them to keep watch while He prayed. Instead, they fell sleep!

Read Mark 14 v 37-42

and compare the three disciples with Jesus.

JESUS	DISCIPLES
Tired, weak and upset (v34).	They were very tired (v40).
Really needed to watch and pray.	Really needed to watch and pray.

Similar, but they acted in totally different ways

JESUS	DISCIPLES
Talked to God (v39).	Kept falling asleep! (v40)
God heard His prayer and gave Him the strength He needed.	Disobeyed Jesus and were open to temptation (v38).

Like these three disciples, all Christians need to **WATCH** and **PRAY**. The devil is always trying to tempt us to do wrong.

So we need to **WATCH OUT** for anything that might cause us to disobey God. And we need to **PRAY**, asking God to help us obey Him.

Think!

What things are you tempted by? (eg: cheating at school, treating your parents badly)

_____

_____

_____

_____

Pray

Ask God to help you to watch out for the devil's temptations. Ask Him to help you to fight the things you wrote down.

WEIRD WORDS

Simon/Peter
Both names refer to the same disciple! The one Jesus said would disown him three times.

Son of Man
Jesus was both God's Son and a human being!

God's plan gone **wrong?**

9

Mark
14 v 43-52

Jesus is in the garden of Gethsemane late at night.

Suddenly, the silence is disturbed, as an angry crowd comes to capture Jesus...

WEIRD WORDS

Chief priests, teachers of the law and elders
Religious leaders who plotted to have Jesus killed

Rabbi
Teacher

Rebellion
Battle against the people in charge

Read Mark 14 v 43-52

What a disaster! At first sight, it looks like everything has gone wrong. Judas has turned against Jesus; Jesus has been captured; and Jesus' friends have deserted Him. How could this be part of God's rescue plan???

1. Judas the betrayer

Fill in the vowels (aeiou) to show what Jesus had said back in Mark 14 v 18.

> **One of y __ __ will**
> **b __ tr __ y m __.**

Who came with the angry mob to arrest Jesus?

> **J __ d __ s**

Jesus knew that Judas was going to betray Him. It was all part of God's rescue plan!

2. Jesus captured

> **He was d __ sp __ s __ d and**
> **r __ j __ ct __ d by**
> **m __ nk __ nd, a man of**
> **s __ ff __ r __ ng, and**
> **familiar with p __ __ n.**
> **(Isaiah 53 v 3)**

Jesus was arrested by the angry mob even though He had done nothing wrong! But Jesus knew He had to be arrested, tortured and killed. It was all part of God's rescue plan. The Old Testament Scriptures (Mark 14 v 49), like Isaiah, had said it would happen!

3. The disciples run away

What did Jesus say back in Mark 14 v 27?

> **Y __ __ w __ ll __ ll**
> **f __ ll __ w __ y**

What happened when Jesus was arrested (v50)?

> **Everyone d __ s __ rt __ d**
> **him and fl __ d**

Jesus had said the disciples would desert Him, and they did! Yet it was all part of God's great rescue plan!

Pray!

Jesus had to suffer and die to rescue us from sin. Spend time thanking God for His perfect plan to rescue us.

The truth from **Ruth**

**Ruth
1 v 1-5**

Today we start reading the great Bible book of Ruth.

We'll meet Ruth, her mother-in-law Naomi and the rich and powerful Boaz.

And we'll learn more about God and His perfect plan for His people.

WEIRD WORDS

Judges
God gave His people judges to lead them

Ephrathites
From an area called Ephrathah

Background info

• Look up Judges 21 v 25. God's people were doing what THEY wanted, not what GOD wanted.

• The action begins in the country of Moab.

• Moab was an enemy of God and God's people, the Israelites.

Time to meet the family...

Read Ruth 1 v 1-5

What a depressing start!

Fill in the blanks to show what happened to Naomi's family.

There was a
f_____ in Israel
(v1). Naomi's husband
E_____ died (v3).
Naomi's sons M_____
and _____ion sadly
died too (v5).

But this family wasn't perfect.

Fill in the blanks to show how they had disobeyed God.

Elimelek and Naomi went
to live in the country of
M_____ (v1). Their sons
married two M_____
women (v4).

That doesn't sound so bad, but Moab was a no-go area for God's people. The Moabites (the people who lived in Moab) didn't love God and worshipped fake gods instead. Living in Moab would make it hard to keep living God's way and serving Him.

Pray!

We live in a world where most people don't live God's way. Ask God to help you stand out as a follower of Jesus. Pray that you won't give in and live for yourself like everyone else does. Pray that you would serve God and not go along with the crowd.

Tomorrow we'll find out what happens next to the three widows...

Home time

Read Ruth 1 v 6-7

Poor Naomi. Alone in the foreign country of Moab with no husband and no sons. It's no surprise that she wanted to move back home to her own people and country. Especially since there was now plenty of food again in Judah.

Read verses 8-13

What did Naomi want Orpah and Ruth to do?

Go back to Judah with her ☐

Wait for her to have more sons for them to marry ☐

Go back to their own families ☐

Naomi really loved her two daughters-in-law, and now they were all she had left.

But unselfishly, she wanted the best for them. Naomi thought they would be happiest if they stayed in Moab to begin new lives.

Action!

How can you put other people first this week?

_____

_____

_____

_____

Will you ask God to help you actually do it?

Look again at verses 8-9

Who is Naomi hoping will look after Ruth and Orpah?

The L__ __ __

Naomi knew that God controlled everything. But things had turned out badly for her. So she thought God was now against her (v13). Later, we'll see if she was right...

Pray!

Ever blamed God for bad stuff happening or got angry with Him? Then say sorry to Him. Ask God to help you trust Him to do what's best even when things seem bad.

WEIRD WORDS

Judah
Part of Israel, where God's people lived. It's where Naomi was from.

Ruth remains

**Ruth
1 v 14-18**

Naomi is going back to Judah.

She wants her daughters-in-law to leave her and go back to their families in Moab.

What will Ruth and Orpah do?

There are loads of decisions we have to make in life. Some are more important than others...

> **What shall I eat for breakfast?**

> **Should I watch that horror movie or not?**

> **Which school subjects shall I choose?**

It's big decision time for Orpah and Ruth. Will they stay in their own country, Moab, or go to Judah with Naomi?

Read Ruth 1 v 14-18

_____ went back to her own family and gods.

_____ went with Naomi to Judah.

Read the verses again

See how serious Ruth was about staying with Naomi.

Fill in the boxes below from verses 16 and 17 to show what she said.

Where you ☐

I will ☐

Where you ☐

I will ☐

Your ☐

will be my ☐

Your ☐

will be my ☐

Where you ☐

I will ☐

What about you? Some decisions are more important than others. And this is one of the most important ones.

Will you GO BACK to your old sinful ways?	Or will you GO ON, living for the only true God?

Talk to God right now about your answer and ask for His help.

Ruth
1 v 19-22

Imagine how Naomi's old friends would feel when they heard the news that she was coming home.

Feeling empty

Read Ruth 1 v 19-22

In Bible times, a person's name often described them.

> Naomi means pleasant. Her life had once been happy.

> **She now wanted to be called M_____ which means b_____ (v20).**
>
> Naomi's life was no longer pleasant. She had lost her husband and sons.

*Fill in the blanks from the word pool to describe Naomi's life **before** she went away, and **now** that she's returned.*

empty   hope

full   afflicted   sons

husband   no hope

BEFORE

Naomi went away f_____

She had a _____

and two _____

She was full of _____

NOW

Naomi felt e_____

She said she'd been

_____ by God

She had _____ _____

Naomi could see no hope. But Naomi still hoped that God, who controls everything, could be kind to Ruth and Orpah (v 8-9).

You couldn't blame God if that was how He left things for Naomi. But in chapter 2 we start to see how God did amazing things for Naomi and Ruth.

Wow!

Sometimes things in our lives seem hopeless. But not only is God in control, He loves to show us love and kindness.

Pray!

Say sorry to God for the times when you haven't trusted Him. Thank Him that He is control and His plans always work out even when things seem bad.
Tell God about anything that's getting you down. Ask Him to sort it out. And keep asking, it may not happen right away!

Glean fingers

**Ruth
2 v 1-7**

Naomi and Ruth had no money and no husbands to go out and work. What would they do???

Read Ruth 2 v 1-7

Ruth went out to earn some food for Naomi and herself. Gleaning wasn't easy work, out in the hot sun all day, but Ruth was prepared to do it.

Whose fields did Ruth gather in?

What was he like? Use the code to fill in the fact file.

How did this happen?

a) Just a coincidence ☐

b) Crafty Ruth knew who owned the field ☐

c) God was taking care of Ruth and Naomi ☐

The answer is c!

WEIRD WORDS

Man of standing
Wealthy and well-respected

Clan of Elimelek
Family of Naomi's husband

Moabite
Woman from the country Moab

Glean
Picking up the grain that the workers left behind

Harvesters
Workers gathering crops

Overseer
Man in charge

Sheaves
Bundles

Boaz – the facts

A _ _ _ _ _ _ _

of Naomi's husband.

He was _ _ _ _.

But he was also _ _ _ _

and _ _ _ _ _.

The field that Ruth gleaned in just happened to belong to one of Naomi's relatives.

Wow!

With God, there are no coincidences. He's in control of everything and He looks after those who love Him.

Pray!

Thank God that He is in total control of what happens in our lives. Thank God that we can always turn to Him for help.

A	B	C	D	E	G	H	I	K	L	N	O	R	T	V	Y	Z

Two of a kind

Ruth and Naomi are so poor that Ruth is having to gather up leftover grain.

Ruth is amazed to discover she is gathering in a relative's field!

What will happen next?

WEIRD WORDS

Glean
Gather crops

Refuge
Protection, safety

Sheaves
Bundles of barley or wheat

Reprimand / Rebuke
Tell her off

Read Ruth 2 v 8-12

Boaz was very kind to Ruth because he had seen how loyal she was to Naomi. *What else did Boaz say to Ruth (v12)? Fill in the vowels please.*

> **May you be r__w__rd__d by the L__rd under whose w__ngs you have found r__f__ge and pr__t__cti__n**

Wow!

God was protecting Ruth, just like a bird protects her babies under her wings. God looks after all His people, Christians. Even though bad things may happen to them, God is always in control and one day they will be safe with Him for ever!

Surely Boaz was only kind to Ruth because he had to obey God's rules, which said that poor people could gather up leftover grain.

Nope! Read verses 13-16

How was Boaz even kinder than the law said he had to be?

1. At lunchtime he gave Ruth br__ __d, v__n__g__r and roasted gr__in (v14).

2. Ruth could gather among the sh__ __ves, not just around the edges (v15).

3. Boaz told his workers to drop extra stalks from their b__ndles for Ruth (v16).

Action!

Do you go out of your way to treat people the way God wants? Below, write down how you're going to help people THIS WEEK.

_____

_____

_____

_____

Pray!

Ask God to help you do the things you've written down.

Guardian what???

**Ruth
2 v 17-23**

What a great day Ruth has been having.

Boaz let her gather loads more barley than she could have imagined.

Ruth hurried home to share all the food and good news with Naomi...

WEIRD WORDS

Threshed
Separated the grain (good bits) from the straw

Ephah
About 22 litres or 13kg

Read Ruth 2 v 17-18

How much did Ruth gather?

About _____

of _____ (v17)

and the food I_____

o_____ from lunch (v18)

An ephah is about two and a half buckets. Not bad for a day's work!

Read verses 19-23

Guardian-redeemer (v20)

A guardian-redeemer had to look after his relatives. His job was to buy back (redeem) his relative's property for them. Or to marry a widow (like Ruth) to make sure she had children to carry on the family. In short, a guardian-redeemer is exactly what Naomi and Ruth needed.

JESUS was the best redeemer ever! He died on the cross to pay the price for our sins. He bought us back for God!

Naomi wasn't stupid. She knew that someone must have been looking after Ruth. And Naomi realised that it wasn't just Boaz who was looking after them.

Who else (v20)?

The L_____

Naomi had thought that her life had all gone wrong (look back at Ruth 1 v 21). Now she was beginning to see how God had never forgotten her.

Wow!

Even when life seems rotten, God never abandons His people. He is always looking after them.

Pray!

What things in your life can you thank God for?

_____

_____

_____

_____

Go on then, thank Him!

Have you done any of the things you wrote down yesterday yet?

Popping the question

**Ruth
3 v 1-13**

*What next for
Ruth???*

WEIRD WORDS

Winnowing
Getting rid of
unwanted bits

Threshing-floor
Where the
winnowing
happened

**Guardian-
redeemer**
See yesterday's
Discover!

Noble character
Good, caring, godly

Redeem
Buy back. Look
after Ruth.

Read Ruth 3 v 1-4

Naomi wanted Ruth to marry Boaz,
so she told Ruth what to do.

*Uncovering his feet sounds weird,
but read **every 2nd letter** to find
out what Ruth was really saying.
Start with the **top W**.*

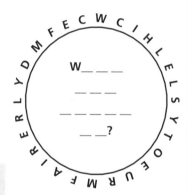

W _ _ _
_ _ _
_ _ _ _
_ _?

Read verses 5-6

Ruth must have been nervous, but
she did everything Naomi said.

Think!

God had a plan to look
after Naomi and Ruth, but Ruth had
to do something to make it work.
Are you willing to follow God's
plans, even when it means doing
something really hard?

Read verses 7-11

Brilliant news! Boaz wants to marry
Ruth! But there is still a problem...

Read verses 12-13

There's another kinsman who is
an even closer relative. If he wants
to, he has the right to marry Ruth
instead of Boaz...

So Boaz will have to wait to find out
if he can marry Ruth. And we will
have to wait to find out too...

Pray!

Ask God to help you be more like
Ruth, willing to serve Him even
when it's really hard.

Pray again!

And ask God to help you be more
like Boaz too, careful to do what's
right even if you'd rather not.

Wait training

Ruth
3 v 14-18

News update.

Ruth slept at Boaz's feet, to show she wanted to marry him.

Boaz wants to marry Ruth. Yay!

But... Boaz might not be allowed to marry Ruth. Oh no!

She might have to marry someone else.

Read Ruth 3 v 14-18

Boaz sent Ruth home with another gift of food to share with Naomi.

How much did he give Ruth this time?

_____ **measures**

of _____

Even though he must have been sooo excited, Boaz was still being practical. In his hurry to get things sorted out (and hopefully marry Ruth!), he didn't forget to help out Ruth and Naomi.

Next, Boaz would go to meet the other relative of Naomi to find out which of them would get to marry Ruth.

At least Boaz could do something about it. Poor Ruth could only sit and wait (v18). Often waiting for something to happen is really tough.

Think!

What do you find it hard to wait for? Your birthday? Holidays? Your Geography lesson to end? Waiting for God to answer prayer and change things can be hard too.

Think of some things that you find it hard to wait for.

_____

_____

_____

_____

_____

_____

Wow!

God is in control of our lives. Sometimes we have to be patient and wait for Him to answer our prayers.

Pray!

Say sorry to God for the times when you're too impatient to wait for Him to do something. Ask Him to help you know when He wants you to act, and when He wants you to wait.

Tomorrow we'll find out if Boaz gets to marry Ruth...

Who'll marry Ruth???

Ruth
4 v 1-6

Will Boaz be able to marry Ruth?

Or will her closer relative claim his right to marry her?

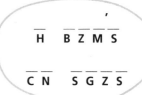

Boaz wasn't in the mood to hang about. Immediately he went to the town gate to wait for the other guardian-redeemer to show up. (The town gate was where most business was done.)

Read Ruth 4 v 1-4

To fill in the conversation, go forward one letter (A=B, B=C, Z=A etc).

__ __ __ __ __   '
H   B Z M S

__ __   __ __ __ __
C N   S G Z S

__ __ __ __   __ __ __
V H K K   X N T

__ __ __   __ __ __ __
A T X   A Z B J
                '
__ __ __ __ __ __
M Z N L H R

__ __ __ __?
K Z M C

__   __ __ __ __
H   V H K K

Read verses 5-6

__ __ __   __ __ __
A T S   X N T

__ __ __ __   __ __ __ __
V H K K   Z K R N

__ __ __ __   __ __
G Z U D   S N

__ __ __ __ __
L Z Q Q X

__ __ __ __
Q T S G

Phew! Boaz must have been relieved. Now he could buy back the land, and more importantly, marry Ruth!

The other guardian-redeemer was no good to Ruth. He was only interested in the land. She needed Boaz, the redeemer who wanted to love her and care for her.

Wow!

That's the kind of redeemer that Jesus is. He died on the cross to pay the price for His people's sins. AND He loves us so much that He wants to know us personally!

WEIRD WORDS

Elders
Leaders

Redeem
Buy back

Estate
His property, land and possessions

Seal the deal

**Ruth
4 v 7-12**

*Ruth's closer
relative agreed
to let Boaz marry
her.*

*It's time to seal
the deal...*

WEIRD WORDS

Redemption
Buying back

**Legalising
transactions**
Sealing the deal,
making it official

Rachel and Leah
They both had lots of
children

Offspring
Children

Perez
An ancestor of
Boaz, and from an
important family

Today, to make deals final and
official, people give each other
contracts. And handshakes. Things
were the same in Boaz's day. Well,
almost the same...

Read Ruth 4 v 7-10

What did the relative give
Boaz to seal the deal?

_____

That seems a bit weird to us.

But the important thing was that
Boaz made sure that everyone knew
he was marrying Ruth and keeping
her family line going.

The people were witnesses that both
the land and Ruth now belonged
to Boaz.

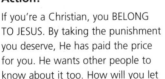

Action!

If you're a Christian, you BELONG
TO JESUS. By taking the punishment
you deserve, He has paid the price
for you. He wants other people to
know about it too. How will you let
your friends and family know you
belong to Jesus?

_____

_____

_____

_____

Read verses 11-12

The locals were so happy! They
wanted God to bless Ruth and Boaz
and give them lots of children to
continue the family line.

Wow!

Other believers will be
thrilled when they see that you really
do belong to Jesus. Hopefully they
will pray for God to bless you and
make your life really useful to Him.
Who knows how many people will
be added to God's family through
what God does in your life?!

Think & pray!

How does all this talk about
belonging to God make you feel?
Excited? Scared? Maybe you're
not part of God's family yet. Or
you're not living for Him as much
as you could do. Talk to God
about it now.

Ruth
4 v 13-22

We're coming to the end of the book of Ruth.

It's a story full of happy endings!

Down the line

Read Ruth 4 v 13-17

To see how things turned out for Ruth and Naomi, fill in the blanks using the word pool.

enemy	husband	new
Jesus	God's	family
Trusted	enemy	Blamed
baby	continued	friend

PERSON	BEFORE	AFTER
Naomi	All her f_____ died B_____ God	T_____ God The family line c_____
Ruth	Her h_____ died An e_____ of God's people	A n_____ husband and new b_____ Part of G_____ family (the Israelites)

But it's not just a happy ending for Naomi and Ruth. It's a happy ending for us too!

Read verses 18-22

What's that got to do with us?

→

Now read Matthew 1 v 1, 5-6 and 16

This family line that God so carefully kept going is the family line of...

J_____ the M_____

WEIRD WORDS

Conceive
Become pregnant

Renew your life
Give you a new lease of life in your old age

Sustain you
Keep you going

Messiah/Christ
God's chosen King

Life had seemed hopeless for Naomi. But now she could see how God's plan for her and Ruth had worked out.

We see how God's plan for Ruth and Naomi includes us too. Jesus was born into that family line. God sent Him so that anyone who trusts in Him can have their wrongs forgiven.

*Can you fill in the chart below for **you**?*

PERSON	BEFORE	AFTER
	An e_____ of God	God's f_____ saved by J_____

Mark: God's rescue plan

Mark
14 v 53-65

Today we jump back into Mark's book about Jesus. When we left it, Jesus had just been arrested by the Jewish leaders. They carried Him off to their court, hoping to sentence Jesus to death.

Read Mark 14 v 53-59

What they were doing was totally wrong...

- It was illegal to have a court at night-time.

- The evidence against Jesus was made up!

- They were desperate to kill Jesus, despite having no evidence against Him.

- Anyway, it was illegal for the Jewish court to send anyone to death!

Jesus had done nothing wrong. He was God's **perfect** Son.

Read verses 60-62

Then complete the conversation.

> **Are you the _____,**
> **Son of _____**
> **_____?**

> **I am. And you will see the _____ sitting at God's side and coming on the _____**
> **_____**

Wow!

Jesus told everyone who He is. He is the Messiah, the King who would rescue God's people. He is God's Son! And one day, everyone will see Jesus return as King!

Read verses 63-65

The Jewish leaders decided that Jesus was lying. Mark wrote his book so that people would know who Jesus really was. Read the Wow! section again, so you get it.

Pray!

Jesus is God's Son! Jesus wants to rescue us! Ask God to help you learn, understand and believe the truth about Jesus as you read the rest of Mark's book.

WEIRD WORDS

Chief priests, elders, teachers of the law
Jewish leaders

Sanhedrin
Jewish court

Testimony
Evidence

The Messiah
The Rescuer sent by God

Blessed One / Mighty One
God

Son of Man
Jesus

Blasphemy
Claiming to be God, a serious crime for Jews

Prophesy!
Go on, predict who hits you!

Peter panics

Mark
14 v 66-72

Remember how Peter boasted that he would never let Jesus down? (Back in Mark 14 v 29-31)

Let's see if Peter lives up to his word...

WEIRD WORDS

Nazarene
Someone from Nazareth, Jesus' home town

Galilean
Someone from the area of Galilee (where Nazareth was)

Disown/deny
Pretending not to know someone

When Jesus was arrested and taken to His trial, Peter followed at a distance.

Read Mark 14 v 66-72

Jesus had warned his disciples that He would be captured by the chief priests. Now it had really happened. Jesus said His friends would leave him, but they all said they wouldn't. Especially Peter.

But Peter panicked. What did the servants say that scared him so much?

v67:

v69:

Jesus had said: *"Before the cockerel crows twice, you will disown me three times"*. Everything Jesus predicted, came true.

Fill in the verse numbers for each one.

Peter denied Jesus once
Verse _____

Peter denied Jesus again
Verse _____

Peter denied Jesus a third time
Verse _____

The cockerel crowed twice
Verse _____

Too late, Peter remembered what Jesus had said. He was so ashamed, he burst into tears.

Think & pray!

Have you ever denied that you have anything to do with Jesus? If so, say sorry. And ask God to help you to stand up for Jesus in front of your friends the next time you get a chance.

Tough trial

**Mark
15 v 1-5**

*The Sanhedrin
(Jewish court)
accused Jesus
of all sorts of
terrible things.*

*But there was
no evidence
against Jesus,
because He had
done nothing
wrong!*

WEIRD WORDS

Elders
Leaders

Bound Jesus
Tied Him up

Low esteem
Thought lowly of
him

Infirmities
Weaknesses

**Smitten/
Afflicted**
Made to suffer

Read Mark 15 v 1

The religious leaders wanted to
kill Jesus, but they didn't have the
power to sentence Jesus to death.
So they handed Him over to Pilate,
the local Roman governor. They
hoped that Pilate would find Jesus
guilty and send Him to His death.

Read verses 2-5

> **Jesus is K_____
> of the J_____
> He is the perfect King sent
> by God to rescue His people!**

Amazingly, Jesus didn't argue with
their false accusations. But it's not
so surprising when you...

... Read Isaiah 53 v 3-7

**Isaiah wrote this 700 years
before Jesus came to earth! Yet
he described exactly what would
happen. Even the way Jesus
behaved during His trial! (v7)**

So why did Jesus accept it all in
silence? Why did He have to suffer
and die? Good old Isaiah tells us
that as well!

Check out verses 5-6 again

Don't be put off by the long words!
Iniquities and transgressions mean
sins.

---

*Who did Jesus go through all this
for? Leave the spaces blank until
you reach the end of the page.*

> **He was pierced for
> _____ transgressions,
> He was crushed for
> _____ iniquities.
> The punishment that
> brought _____ peace
> was on Him.
> And by His wounds
> _____ is healed.**

Jesus' death was punishment for all
the sins of His people.

Think!

Do you believe that Jesus died as
a punishment for YOUR sins, so
that YOU can be forgiven? Have
you said sorry for the wrongs
you've done, and asked Jesus to
forgive you?

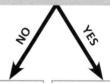

NO / **YES**

| **Why not?** **Do you want to? Ask God to help you make a wise decision.** | **Put your name in the spaces. And give God a massive thank you!** |

25

Things get worse

Mark
15 v 6-15

The people must choose between two men.

One gets set free; the other is sentenced to death...

WEIRD WORDS

The Festival
Passover (see Day 3)

Rebels
People fighting against the Roman rulers

Uprising
People getting together to fight the Romans

Crucify him
Kill him by nailing him to a wooden cross

The Choice	
Barabbas	**Jesus**
Rebel	Peacemaker
Thief	Healer
Murderer	Life-giver

Read Mark 6 v 6-8

Write "Jesus" or "Barabbas" or "Don't know, mate!" to answer these questions.

Who had broken the law?

_____

Who should the chief priests have spoken against?

_____

Who should Pilate have punished?

_____

Who deserved to die?

_____

Now read verses 9-15

Who did the people reject?

_____

Who did the chief priests turn the crowd against?

_____

Who was sentenced to death?

_____

The Jewish leaders were envious of Jesus, but that's not why Jesus died. Nor was it because Pilate gave in to the crowd.

Wow!
Jesus didn't speak against the wrong accusations because He knew He had to die. It was all part of God's rescue plan! His plan to rescue us from punishment for our sin!

Pray!

Even when the murder plot looked to be working, God was always in control. Thank God that He is always in control, and that His plans work out.

Rough stuff

Warning!

Today's Bible bit is horrific and upsetting.

But it's the truth about Jesus and what He went through for us.

WEIRD WORDS

Flogged
Whipped

Crucified
Nailed to a cross

Paid homage
Mocked Jesus by pretending to show great respect for Him

Read Mark 15 v 15-20

Fill in all the missing words and verse numbers.

He was flogged (verse _____)

The Roman whip was made of strips of leather with pieces of lead and bone attached to them. It was designed to bite into the flesh. Nasty.

Have you ever been hit with a school tie? It can really hurt. Well this was a thousand times worse.

They made Jesus a c_____ of t_____ (v17)

Even a splinter can be painful! But this crown was made of lots of sharp and painful thorns which dug into Jesus' skin.

They spat on Him (verse _____) and mocked and teased Him (verse _____)

Have you ever been beaten up or teased? It's a rotten feeling, isn't it?

Think!

Is there anything in your life that hurts? Maybe you're teased and hassled at school?

_____

_____

_____

Wow!

When you pray to Jesus, you're speaking to someone who knows just what that feels like. Jesus understands all the pain and hurt you feel, because He has felt it too!

Pray!

Tell Jesus about any hurt or anger you feel. You can talk to Him about it, and ask Him to comfort you. He will. And thank Jesus for going through all of that suffering for you.

Mark
15 v 21-32

The amazing life of Jesus, God's Son, seems to be coming to a sad and painful end...

WEIRD WORDS

Cyrene
City in Africa, a long way from Jerusalem

Myrrh
Perfume

Cast lots
Threw dice to make a decision

King of Israel
They were mocking Jesus. But He really was the King of God's people, Israel.

Cross words

Read Mark 15 v 21-25

"And they crucified Him."

WEIRD WORDS
Crucifixion
It was the cruellest possible death, used only for slaves and the worst criminals. The victim was stripped, had sharp nails hammered through his hands and feet, and then was left to die slowly and painfully.

And this is what Jesus went through. On purpose. For you and me. To rescue us from sin.

Read verses 26-27
Fill in the sign from verse 26.

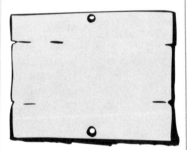

This was meant to be a joke, but it was totally true! The Jewish people were crucifying their King. Not only **their** King, but the King of the whole world.

Read verses 29-32
How did people react when they saw Jesus nailed to the cross? Circle the words that best describe them.

sad   insulting

ashamed   unkind

sarcastic   sympathetic

loving   jeering

vicious

The chief priests and other religious leaders were pleased. Jesus seemed so weak. They thought this was their hour of victory... but they were dead wrong!

Wow!

It wasn't weakness that kept Jesus on the cross, but strength. The strength of His love for people like you and me. His enemies didn't realise that on the cross, Jesus showed...
not weakness, but STRENGTH!
not failure, but SUCCESS!
not defeat, but VICTORY!

And Jesus was about to beat death once and for all.
More tomorrow...

In the dark

When the sky is dark, it usually means that it's night-time.

Or maybe a thunderstorm is on the way.

But to Jesus, in the last few hours of His life, when the skies turned dark it meant something very different...

Read Mark 15 v 33-37

It was only midday when the sky turned black. Was this just weird weather? No way!

*What did Jesus cry out? (v34)
Use the code to work it out.*

So what did Jesus mean?

> **The terrifying darkness was a sign that God was punishing Jesus.**

Jesus took responsibility for all of our sins.

> **God hates sin, and so could no longer be close to Jesus. God had abandoned Him.**

Even worse, His Father had to punish Jesus for all that terrible sin.

> **But Jesus didn't stop trusting God. In fact, by dying, He showed how much He trusted and obeyed His Father.**

But that's not the end of the story! More tomorrow...

Think & pray!

Jesus went through all of that for you and me! Spend time talking to God, responding to what He's done for you. Tell Him exactly how you feel.

WEIRD WORDS

Forsaken
Abandoned

Elijah
Prophet from 800 years earlier. Some people believed that Elijah would rescue you in time of trouble.

A	D	E	F	G	H	K	M	N	O	R	S	U	V	W	Y

That's **torn** it!

Mark
15 v 37-38

Jesus died on a cross, over 2000 years ago. That's a long time ago.

How could something so long ago be important to us now, 2000 years later?

WHAT'S IT ALL ABOUT???

By the way, if you'd like the free e-booklet *What's it all about?*, email discover@ thegoodbook. co.uk or check out www. thegoodbook. co.uk/contact-us to find our UK mailing address.

When Jesus died, something really weird happened.

Read Mark 15 v 37-38

Fill in the gaps please!

The _____ of the _____ was torn in two from _____ to _____.

Curtain facts!

The curtain in the temple had always been a barrier, separating the people from the *Most Holy Place*.

That's where God had been present in a special way.

Only the high priest could go through the curtain to God. And that was only once a year, and only with a special sacrifice — a gift for God.

The curtain stopped ordinary people from getting close to God.

The curtain was destroyed when Jesus died!

Er, so what's that mean then?

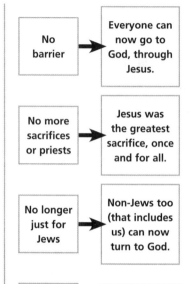

No barrier	→	Everyone can now go to God, through Jesus.
No more sacrifices or priests	→	Jesus was the greatest sacrifice, once and for all.
No longer just for Jews	→	Non-Jews too (that includes us) can now turn to God.
No other way	→	Jesus is the only way to God.

Pray!

Praise and thank God that we can now go straight to Him. We can get to know God! Jesus has made it possible! We just need to believe and trust that Jesus died to take our punishment.

Dead and buried

WEIRD WORDS

Centurion
Commander in the Roman army

Mary Magdalene
Woman who Jesus had healed

Sabbath
Saturday — the Jewish holy day when people would rest and worship God

Council
Religious leaders

Kingdom of God
Living in God's kingdom means living with Him as the King in charge of your life

Jesus has died. He has taken the punishment for the wrongs we have done. Surely that's the end of the story? Not yet it's not...

Read Mark 15 v 39
What did the Roman soldier figure out about Jesus?

Surely Jesus was the

_____

That's exactly right. Do **you** praise Jesus for being God's Son?

*Are you brave? It's time to take the Toughness Test! Answer **YES** or **NO** to each question.*

1. Are afraid of the dark? _____

2. Do you feel queasy at the sight of blood? _____

3. Would you stick by a friend, even it meant risking arrest or death? _____

4. Do you dare to tell your friends about Jesus? _____

It's easy to *sound* brave. Remember how the disciples claimed they'd never leave Jesus? (Mark 14 v 31)

But when it came to the crunch, they were all cowards and ran away.

But some of Jesus' followers were brave.

Read verses 40-41
These women were braver than the disciples! Jesus mattered so much to them.

Read verses 42-47
Joseph had a lot to lose. He was a member of the Sanhedrin, the Jewish court that had plotted to kill Jesus. He was expected to hate Jesus. But he was really a secret follower of Jesus! He bravely went to Pilate to ask for Jesus' body so that he could bury it properly. He took a risk because he loved Jesus.

Pray!

Do you love Jesus? Ask God to give you courage like these women and Joseph, so that you live for Jesus, no matter what the risk.

Jesus' followers didn't realise what amazing thing would happen next. Find out tomorrow...

Where's he gone?

31

**Mark
16 v 1-8**

Even though Jesus had said He would beat death, no-one really expected it to happen.

This would be the most important day in history!

(Many experts think v 9-20 aren't part of the original Gospel so we'll miss them out.)

The Jewish leaders must have been relieved to have finally got rid of Jesus. But it brought great sadness to these women now on their way to His tomb.

Read Mark 16 v 1-3

These women had no doubts that Jesus had died. They had seen it themselves. And they knew He was buried because they had been watching when His body was put in the tomb, and the massive stone was rolled across the entrance.

But how would they move it???

Read verses 4-8

No problem! What great news did the angel have? Write down *every third letter* to find out.

**KAHFOEGNHWRA
PXSZTRBUIPUSCVESMN
OXHIKEDHIQJSDYNRFO
LGTOSHXVEOWRAAE**

— —   — — —

— — — — —!

— —   — —

— — —

— — — —!

Mary, Mary and Salome were terrified and amazed that God had raised Jesus back to life.

Wow!

Death was not the end! Jesus has come back to life to live for ever! So if we've asked Him to forgive our wrongs, then we don't have to go to hell for ever. We can have everlasting life with Him!

Pray!

Thank and praise Jesus for taking the punishment and beating death for YOU!

Would you like a free e-booklet explaining more?
Choose from *Why did Jesus rise?* and *How to become a Christian.*
Email
discover@thegoodbook.co.uk
or check out
www.thegoodbook.co.uk/contact-us
to find our UK mailing address.

WEIRD WORDS

Anoint
Put perfume on Jesus' body

Bewildered
Confused

Genesis: Dreamer Drama

Genesis 37 v 1-4

In the last few issues of Discover, we've been working our way through Genesis.

We've read all about how God created the universe.

And we've read the stories of Abraham, his son Isaac, and grandson Jacob.

God made the same 3 promises to them all.

Go back one letter to reveal God's promises.

1. _ _ _ _
M B O E

God promised to give their family (the Israelites) the land of Canaan to live in.

2. _ _ _ _ _ _ _ _
D I J M E S F O

God promised that their family would grow into a great nation. The Israelites were God's special people.

3. _ _ _ _ _ _ _ _
C M F T T J O H

God promised to bless the world, using this family. That would happen when Jesus was born into this family.

As we join the story in Genesis chapter 37, Jacob and his family are **living in Canaan**, and his **family is growing**. God is keeping His promises! As we read the stories of Jacob and his son, Joseph, we'll see more of God's great promises.

Read Genesis 37 v 1-4

This is no perfect family! Jacob treated his son Joseph better than his other kids. And they hated Joseph. Yet God made great promises to this sinful family!

Pray!

In the same way, God promises great things, through Jesus, to sinners like us. Thank God for His great kindness. And pray you'll learn from Joseph.

Figure of hate

Genesis 37 v 5-11

Joseph is the favourite son of his father, Jacob.

But his brothers hate him and don't have a kind word to say to him.

Dreams can be weird. What's the strangest dream you've had?

Joseph had a bizarre dream...

Read Genesis 37 v 5-8

This was an unusual dream because it had a real meaning. Joseph's brothers knew it was about them all bowing down to him. That really annoyed them!

Read verses 9-11

Do you think Joseph's dreams will come true? Will his family bow down to him?

Yes/No _____

Well, you'll have to keep reading *Discover* to find out! (The answer is in Genesis 42 if you can't wait.)

How did Joseph's family react to his dreams? (v10-11)

Joseph's dad	His brothers

Joseph had the best coat, he was his dad's fave son, and he seemed to think he was better than his brothers. So did they have a good reason to hate him?

Check out 1 John 3 v 15

What does this verse tell us about God's attitude to hatred?

Think & pray!

Is there anyone you hate or treat really badly?

_____

_____

Ask God to help you love them more and treat them better.

WEIRD WORDS

Binding sheaves of corn
Tying up the bundles of corn they had collected

Rebuked him
Told him off

Brothers and cisterns

Genesis 37 v 12-24

Joseph's brothers hated him because he dreamed they would bow down to him.

Soon they would have the chance to get their revenge.

WEIRD WORDS

Israel
Jacob

Cisterns
Pits/wells where water is stored

Robe
The lovely coat Joseph's dad gave him

Read Genesis 37 v 12-20

Joseph travelled over 60 miles to find his brothers. But what did they say when they saw him coming? *Fill in the blanks (v19-20).*

Here comes that d_____!

Let's k_____ him and t_____ his body into a cistern.

Yeah, we can say that a wild a_____ killed him.

Read verses 21-24

Reuben tried to rescue Joseph.

*Cross out the things he **didn't** say.*

Let's not take his light/life. Don't shed any blood/bleach/blossom. Kick/hit/throw him into this lantern/cistern, but don't lay a hat/hand on him.

Reuben stood up to his brothers, who wanted to kill Joseph.

Action!

What do you need to take a stand against? Circle ones you've seen & add your own...

**friends telling rude jokes
cheating in exams
friends teasing other kids
swearing, using God's name**

_____

_____

Things are looking bad for Joseph.

But...

• God was in control of everything that was happening

• God used Reuben to stop Joseph's brothers killing him

• God had a plan for Joseph's life

Pray!

Thank God that whatever is happening to us, He is in total control! And ask Him to help you speak out against stuff you know is wrong.

Bye bye Joseph

**Genesis
37 v 25-36**

*Joseph's brothers
have thrown him
into a pit. Will
they kill him?*

*(All of today's
missing words
can be found
down the centre
of the page.)*

WEIRD WORDS

Caravan
Group of travellers

**Ishmaelites/
Midianites**
The same group of
merchants (salesmen)

Balm
Healing oil

Myrrh
Beauty oil

20 shekels
230g of silver

Sackcloth
Rough clothes worn
when upset

Read Genesis 37 v 25-30

Joseph's brothers saw a
group of I_____.
Their c_____ were
loaded with s_____
which they were going
to sell in E_____
(v25). One of Joseph's
brothers, J_____,
persuaded the others
not to k_____ Joseph
(v26). So they s_____
Joseph to the Ishmaelite
salesmen for 20 shekels of
s_____ (v28). When
R_____ got back, he
found that J_____
was no longer in the
c_____ (v29).

Read verses 31-35

The brothers killed a
g_____ and dipped
Joseph's r_____ in its
b_____ (v31). They took

animal Ishmaelites blood Jacob cistern Joseph camels Judah comfort kill dead Reuben Egypt robe silver father goat spices sold

it to their f_____,
who thought Joseph
had been killed by a
wild a_____.
J_____ was hugely
upset because he thought
his son Joseph was
d_____. No one could
c_____ him (v35).

Things are looking bad. Joseph's
own brothers have sold him as
a slave. They've also told their
dad that Joseph is dead. And
Joseph's now on his way to a
different country...

But read verse 36

Wow!

Joseph's been sold as a
slave to someone really
important in Egypt. This was
all part of God's great plan for
Joseph. God would use Joseph
to do great things in Egypt. Even
when things seem bad, God's
great plans are working out.

Pray!

Thank God that His plans for us
are perfect. Ask God to use YOU
to serve Him.

Potty for Joseph

Genesis
39 v 1-6

Joseph has been sold as a slave to Potiphar, a very important man in Egypt.

But first, let's see how Joseph's brother Judah is getting on...

WEIRD WORDS

Pharaoh
King of Egypt

Prospered
Was successful

Attendant
Servant

Blessed
God did good things for them

Judah's story

(It's in Genesis chapter 38.) Judah got married and they had three sons. Two of Judah's sons did terrible things and God punished them with death. Judah also messed up, and got his daughter-in-law (Tamar) pregnant. Tamar had twins called Perez and Zerah.

Wow!

What a sinful mess of a family! Amazingly, God still used this family in His great plans! Perez was the great great great etc... grandfather of Jesus! God would keep His promise to bless the world through this family!

Joseph's story
Read Genesis 39 v 1-6

Joseph was now a slave to Potiphar, the captain of Pharaoh's guards. For once, things started going right for Joseph. Everything he did was successful, so Potiphar put Joseph in charge of everything he owned!

*What was the secret of Joseph's success? Find out by taking **every second letter**, starting with the **T** at the top.*

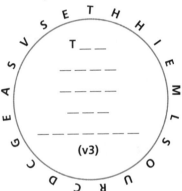

T _ _ _

_ _ _ _ _

_ _ _ _

_ _ _ _ _ _

(v3)

Letters around circle: T H H I E M L S O U R C D G E A S V S E

Think!

When things go well for you and you're successful, do you get big-headed about it? Or do you remember that it's God who gives you success?

Pray!

Think of some of the good things you've done. Spend time thanking God for making these achievements possible.

Joe says no

Genesis 39 v 6-23

After being sold as a slave by his brothers, Joseph found himself with a top job in charge of Potiphar's place in Egypt.

But he was about to get into another tricky situation.

WEIRD WORDS

Hebrew
One of God's people, the Israelites

Make sport
Laugh at

Prison warder
Prison guard

Read Genesis 39 v 6-12

Potiphar's wife was attracted to Joseph, and kept asking him to sleep with her. But Joe said **NO!**

He wouldn't betray his boss Potiphar, or sin against God.

And when things got really tricky, he even ran away!

Go on, steal it! No one will notice.

Let's go and tease Jenny...

Action

What wrong things do friends try to persuade you to do?

_____

_____

_____

_____

Wow!

When people want us to do stuff we know is wrong, we've got to say NO! And if they keep insisting, then we should RUN AWAY from the situation.

Read verses 13-18

Potiphar's wife lied, telling everyone that Joseph had tried to sleep with her! Uh-oh, it looks like Joseph's in trouble again...

Read verses 19-23

Joseph was thrown in prison for a crime he didn't commit. But it wasn't all bad. The prison guard was impressed with Joseph and put him in charge of the other prisoners!

Why did Joseph have so much success? Fill in the first letter of each word to find out.

__ecause __he __ord __as __ith __oseph __nd __ave __im __uccess __n __hatever __e __id (v23)

Wow!

When life gets tough, we often just sulk and feel sorry for ourselves. But God's still with us and He can do amazing things even in bad situations.

Pray!

Thank God that He's always with you. Ask Him to help you say NO! to doing stuff that you know is wrong.

38

Genesis 40 v 1-15

Joseph's been thrown into jail for a crime he didn't commit.

But God is looking after him...

WEIRD WORDS

Cupbearer
Man in charge of Pharaoh's wine

Pharaoh / King of Egypt
The same person

Dejected
Really sad

Vine
Grape plant

Blossomed
Grew flowers

Land of the Hebrews
Canaan, the land God promised to His people

On the grapevine

Read Genesis 40 v 1-8

Pharaoh threw two of his servants in prison with Joseph. One was Pharaoh's baker, the other was his cupbearer, responsible for Pharaoh's wine.

They both had dreams that bothered them.

What did Joseph say to them? (v8)

He knew that only God could tell them what their dreams meant. God was with Joseph, and would help Joe to interpret their dreams!

Think!

God is our Creator, so He knows and understands everything. Is there anyone better to trust? Do you turn to Him when life seems tricky?

Read verses 9-11

*… and cross out the bits that were **not** in the dream.*

I saw a vole/vine/phone in front of me. It had three legs/branches/text messages. As soon as as the buds came out, so did the blossom/bottom, and apes/tapes/grapes grew on it. Pharaoh's cup/cap/cape was in my hand. I squealed/squeezed the grapes into Pharaoh's cup and put it in his head/hand/haddock.

Read verses 12-15

… to find out what the dream means.

The three branches are three days/Daves/dogs. Within three days, Pharaoh will give you your job/dog back. You will fill Pharaoh's pup/cup again, as you used to. When things go well for you mention me to Potiphar/Pharaoh, and get me out of Paris/prison.

God helped Joseph to understand the dream. Maybe God would use this to get Joseph out of prison.

Pray!

Thank God that we can trust Him, even when life seems hard. Thank Him that He can help you to do things you never thought you could do.

**Genesis
40 v 16-23**

*Pharaoh's baker
and cupbearer
are in prison
with Joseph, and
they've both had
weird dreams.*

*Joseph told the
cupbearer that his
dream was good
news.*

*Now it's the
baker's turn...*

WEIRD WORDS

**Favourable
interpretation**
His dream had a
good meaning

Impale
Spear

Bad news, good news

Read Genesis 40 v 16-17

and complete the pic of the baker's
dream.

Read verses 18-19

Oh dear. That's very different
from the cupbearer's dream. God
told Joseph what both dreams
meant. Pharaoh would forgive the
cupbearer, but kill the baker. And
the birds would eat the baker's flesh
— yuck!

Read verses 20-23

Everything happened
exactly as God had
told Joseph it would.
What God promises
always
happens.

Sometimes that's bad
news and sometimes
it's good news...

Bad news

Use the code to reveal the first half
of Romans 6 v 23.

We've all sinned. God has promised
to punish sinners with death. But...

Good news

God promises to forgive anyone
who trusts Jesus to rescue them!

Pray!

Thank God that His words always
come true. Thank Him for His
promise of rescue.

Pharaoh story

**Genesis
41 v 1-16**

Two years have passed, and Joseph is still in prison.

The cupbearer must have forgotten to tell Pharaoh about him.

WEIRD WORDS

Nile
Big river in Egypt

Sleek
Fit and healthy

Gaunt
Really skinny and ill-looking

Shortcomings
Failings

Young Hebrew
Joseph, one of God's special people

Read Genesis 41 v 1-7

What cool dreams! *Try and describe them...*

Cow dream

The first 7 cows were

_____

The second lot were

_____

What happened?

_____

_____

Corny dream

The first 7 ears of corn were

_____

The second lot were

_____

What happened?

_____

_____

Read verses 8-13

No one could tell Pharaoh what his dreams meant. But Pharaoh's cupbearer remembered how Joseph could understand dreams.

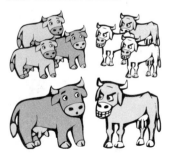

Read verses 14-16

Finally Joseph met Pharaoh. *Complete their conversation.*

I've heard that when you h__ __r a dr__ __m, you c__n __nt__rpr__t it.

I c__nn__t do it. But G__d w__ll give Ph__r__ __h the __nsw__r he wants.

Joseph knew he couldn't do it by himself. But he knew that God would help him to understand Pharaoh's dreams.

Think!

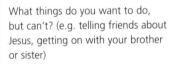

What things do you want to do, but can't? (e.g. telling friends about Jesus, getting on with your brother or sister)

_____
_____
_____
_____

Pray!

God can do anything! Ask Him to help you do the things you've written down.

44

Dreams come true?

**Genesis
41 v 17-36**

Pharaoh wanted
Joseph to tell him
what his weird
dreams meant.

Joseph said that
God would give
him the answer...

Read Genesis 41 v 17-24

*Okay Picasso, draw a pic for each of
Pharaoh's dreams.*

cow dream

corn dream

Wow!

God is in charge! God gave Pharaoh
the dreams, and God knew all about
the famine. God warned Pharaoh
so he could do something about
it. We know that when God says
something, it comes true! He always
keeps His promises.

Now read verses 25-32

Both of the dreams meant the same
thing — there would be seven great
years with loads to eat. Then there
would be seven years of terrible
famine when all the food would run
out. *Fill in Joseph's missing words
from verses 25 and 32.*

_____ has revealed
to Pharaoh what He is
about to do. The matter
has been firmly decided
by _____, and _____
will do it soon.

Read verses 33-36

Joseph told Pharaoh he'd need to
put someone in charge of storing
up food over the next seven years,
so they'd have enough when the
famine kicked in. I wonder who
Pharaoh will choose...

Pray!

We have loads to praise and
thank God for! Thank God that
He is in charge of everything.
Thank Him that He knows
everything that will happen in
your life. Thank Him for always
being with His people (Christians)!

WEIRD WORDS

Abundance
Loads and loads of
crops

Ravage the land
The famine will
wreck the country

Discerning
Making wise
decisions

Commissioners
Men in charge of
food supplies

Spot the **difference**

42

Genesis 41 v 37-46

There will be seven great years in Egypt.

And then there will be seven years of famine.

Remember the sound advice that Joseph gave Pharaoh? (Verses 33-36)

WEIRD WORDS

Signet ring

Giving this ring to someone showed that Pharaoh was pleased with them, and gave them some of his power.

Read Genesis 41 v 37-38

What did Pharaoh see in Joseph (v38)? Go forward one letter (A=B, B=C etc) to find out.

___ ___ ___

S G D

___ ___ ___ ___ ___ ___

R O H Q H S

___ ___   ___ ___ ___

N E   F N C

From the way Joseph acted, and what he said, Pharaoh noticed that God was with him!

Think!

Are you a Christian? If so, do your friends know? Do they notice that God is with you, by the things you say and do?

Action!

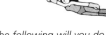

Which of the following will you do to show that God is in your life? Only tick things you're actually going to try.

give up bad language ☐

talk about church more ☐

be nicer to your bro or sis ☐

tell friends you're a Christian ☐

refuse to join in with bullying ☐

tell your friends about Jesus ☐

Important!

Now tell a Christian friend what you've decided to do. They can check up on you and encourage you.

Read verses 39-46

Wow! Pharaoh made Joseph the second most important person in the whole of Egypt! And he did it because he saw that **God** was with Joseph (v39).

Sadly, it doesn't always work that way. Sometimes people will give us more respect for being Christians. But often they will hassle us, tease us or ignore us.

Pray!

Which boxes did you tick?

_____

_____

_____

Ask God to help you do those things, so that your friends and family realise how important God is to you.

Forget me not

**Genesis
41 v 47-57**

*Suzie's fed up
with her brother.*

*He's really nice
to her when he
needs help with
his homework.*

*But the rest
of the time he
pretends she
doesn't exist.*

We often treat God like that.
Only turning to Him when we
need His help. Forgetting Him
the rest of the time.

Was Joseph going to be like that?
Would he still remember God now
that things were going well for him?

Read Genesis 41 v 47-49

Maybe now he was rich and
famous, Joseph would forget about
God.

Read verses 50-52

*What did Joseph name his sons? Go
back one letter (B=A, C=B etc) to
find out.*

— — — — — — —
N B O B T T F I
means

— — — — — —
G P S H F U

Joseph thanked God for being with
him all the time, helping him to
forget all the troubles he'd had.

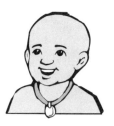

— — — — — —
F Q I S B J N
means

— — — — — — —
G S V J U G V M

Joseph remembered how much God
had given him.

Action!

Quick, grab a spare sheet of paper.
Make a list of things God has given
you and things God has done for
you. You could even turn it into a
poster for your wall, to help you
remember what God has done for
you.

Read verses 53-57

God's plan to save up food for the
famine is working. The people of
Egypt are surviving!

Pray!

Ask God to help you not to forget
Him. Use the list you wrote earlier
to thank God for what He's done
for you.

44

Acts: Spreading the word

Acts

10 v 1-8

Time to dive into the book of Acts. The new Christians are spreading the good news about Jesus everywhere!

But today, let's sneak into a Roman soldier's house...

WEIRD WORDS

Centurion
Commander in the Roman army

Devout and God-fearing
Devoted to God, giving Him the respect He deserves

Tanner
Man who worked with animal skins.

Read Acts 10 v 1-2

and answer these questions about the man mentioned there.

QUESTION TIME!

1. What's his name?

C_____

2. Where does he live?

C_____

3. What's his job?

C_____

But there was also something **unusual** about this man (v2).

Go back one letter to figure out what was so strange about him.

___ ___   ___ ___ ___
I F   X B T

___   ___ ___ ___ ___ ___ ___
B   H F O U J M F

___ ___ ___   ___ ___
C V U   I F

___ ___ ___ ___ ___ ___
Q S B Z F E

___ ___   ___ ___ ___
U P   H P E

Normally Gentiles (non-Jews) worshipped false gods. It was Jews who believed in God. But Cornelius prayed to God regularly (see verse 2).

Read another strange thing that happened in verses 3-6

God answered Cornelius' prayers with a special message from an angel. He was told to ask Peter the disciple to visit him.

How did Cornelius react?

Read verses 7-8

and describe his reaction.

Cornelius might have thought: "There's no point in praying. God won't answer my prayers because I'm not a Jew." But God **did** answer his prayers!

Pray!

Do you ever think *"God won't answer my prayers — I'm not good enough"*? It's not true! God loves to hear us talk to Him and He loves to answer! So talk to God right now!

45

Never say **never** to God

Acts
10 v 9-23

Peter was a Jew, so he followed all the Old Testament laws about food. Peter would never eat animals forbidden by Jewish laws. He would rather starve than eat unclean food.

Read Acts 10 v 9-16

Strange. God told Peter to kill and eat **unclean** animals.

Cornelius, the Roman centurion, saw an angel in a vision.

How did Peter reply (v14)?

Ugh! Not reptiles!!! ☐

Surely not, Lord! ☐

If you say so Lord, then it must be right ☐

The angel told him to invite Peter to his house.

The action now switches to Peter...

What would have been a better answer? Circle it.

So why could Peter now eat unclean food? (See verse 15)

When Jesus died on the cross, He took the place of these Old Testament rules. Peter had to learn that God is willing to accept anyone who trusts in Jesus to save them. Not just Jewish people.

Wow!

Never say NO to God. Sometimes in the Bible, God tells us to do something we've always dreaded. Like telling people about Jesus (Acts 1 v 8). Or something we thought impossible. Like obeying our parents! (Exodus 20 v 12).

Read verses 17-23

It must have been really difficult for Peter. He was going against the Jewish traditions he'd been taught for years. Usually, he would have turned the men away but God had spoken to him. God had told Peter to do unclean things, like spending time with Gentiles.

WEIRD WORDS

Trance
A dreamlike state, where he had a vision

The Spirit
Holy Spirit

Righteous
Living God's way

If God has said it in His Word (the Bible) then it must be right. But if you're unsure about anything the Bible says, it's a good idea to check it out with an older Christian.

Pray!

Say a massive thank you to God for the great news that ANYONE can have their wrongs forgiven by Jesus.

Pete's meet and greet

Read Acts 10 v 24-33

Peter and Cornelius were very different in loads of ways. *Draw arrows to show which description belongs to who. (Two of them belong to both.)*

lived in Caesarea
poor
disciple
staying in Joppa
commander in army
wealthy
obeyed God
Gentile
prayed to God
Jewish

Many Jewish people looked down on Gentiles (non-Jews).

They would have nothing to do with them.

So what's this?

Peter (a Jew) is visiting Cornelius (a Gentile).

Normally, these two men would never have met. They had probably never even heard of each other. But they had two things in common. *What were they? (They're in the list!)*

1.	2.

And that's why they met. Remember Peter's vision, which he was so puzzled over? (See yesterday's *Discover*.) **Read verses 28-29 again.**

Peter now knew what his strange vision meant.
God wanted him to meet with people of **all nations**. Both Jews and Gentiles.
Peter had learned a really important lesson: **the good news of Jesus is for everyone!**

Peter only learned this lesson because he was ready to do what God said.

Pray!

Maybe you're struggling over something you know you should do, but haven't done it yet. Ask God for the courage to obey what He says.

Think!

Is there someone you ignore, who you could talk to about Jesus?

_____

_____

47

Good news all round

Cornelius and his guests are waiting to hear what Peter has to say to them...

Let's listen in too.

Read Acts 10 v 34-43. Twice.

Peter told them the fantastic news about Jesus. *From the word pool, arrange what he said about Jesus in the same order that he said it.*

Appeared to witnesses

Did good   Holy Spirit

Raised from the dead by God

Healed loads of people

Became judge of everyone

JESUS CHRIST

⬇

God gave Him the...

(v38)

⬇

(v38)

⬇

(v38)

⬇

Was killed on the cross (v39)

⬇

(v40)

⬇

(v41)

⬇

(v42)

Before: Peter believed that the gospel message was for Jews only.

Now: God had shown him that the good news of Jesus is for everyone in the world!

Read verse 42

So we should tell **EVERYONE** about Jesus. That's why Peter told Cornelius and his friends all about Jesus.

So does it matter...

what colour your skin is?

how bad you've been?

how wealthy you are?

YES/NO _____

Nope. The good news that Jesus died to forgive our sins is for absolutely everybody.

Read verse 43

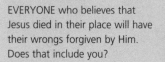

Think!

EVERYONE who believes that Jesus died in their place will have their wrongs forgiven by Him. Does that include you?

WEIRD WORDS

Fear him
Show love and respect for God by living His way

Anointed
God gave Jesus the Holy Spirit to help Him serve His Father

Testify
Tell everyone

48

Sound **proof**

**Acts
10 v 44-48**

*Have you ever
won anything?*

*How could you
prove that you'd
won it?*

_____

_____

_____

If you have a trophy or a certificate,
you could convince me that you had
won it. The trophy would be **proof**.

In today's Bible bit, we're still at
Cornelius' house. God will **prove**
something important to Peter's
Jewish friends. Peter has preached
about Jesus to the Gentiles (non-
Jews) who were there. But would
they believe in Jesus?

Read Acts 10 v 44-46

*What is the **proof** that these
Gentiles really had believed? Fill in
the missing words.*

> The H_____ Spirit came
>
> upon the G_____s
>
> and they sp_____ in
>
> t_____s and
>
> praised G_____

This was the same thing that
happened to loads of Jewish
believers at Pentecost. If you want
a reminder of what happened at
Pentecost, check out **Acts 2 v 1-12.**

The Jews were astonished (v45). But
this was definite **proof** that God
was now with non-Jews too. Jesus
came to save **EVERYONE**, not just
Jewish people.

Read verses 47-48

These people became followers of
Jesus. So they were baptised and
welcomed into God's family.

Think!

When someone you know
becomes a Christian, will you
welcome them into God's family?
How can you do that?

_____

_____

Think again!

Have you got the message yet???
The great news that Jesus died
to save us from our sins is for
EVERYONE.
So are you telling people?

Need some help? For a free fact sheet
on *how to tell your friends about
Jesus*, email
discover@thegoodbook.co.uk
or check out
www.thegoodbook.co.uk/contact-us
to find our UK mailing address.

WEIRD WORDS

**Circumcised
believers**
Jewish believers

**Speaking in
tongues**
Speaking
in different
languages

49

Critical condition

Acts
11 v 1-18

Peter learned that the good news about Jesus was for everyone, not just Jewish people.

WEIRD WORDS

Apostles and the believers
Jewish believers

Circumcised believers
Jewish believers

Uncircumcised
Non-Jews

Repentance that leads to life
Turning from sin to God and eternal life

Back in Jerusalem, trouble was brewing...

Read Acts 11 v 1-3

> **How could you visit Gentiles?! That's against Jewish law!**

The Jewish believers thought this was terrible. They hadn't understood Jesus' instructions to preach the gospel to **everyone**.

Think & pray!

It's easy to avoid parts of the Bible that don't fit in with our ideas. Ask God to change your ideas to fit the Bible, not the other way round!

How do you think Peter will react?

a) Get angry at their criticism
b) Throw rotten fruit at them
c) Explain the whole story

> **Your answer:**

Read verse 4 to find out.

Think!
How do YOU react to unfair criticism?

_____

_____

_____

_____

Read Peter's explanation in verses 5-17

How do you think they reacted to Peter's story?

a) Praised God
b) Didn't believe Peter
c) Threw rotten fruit at him

> **Your answer:**

Read verse 18

They had been sure they were right. But they were humble enough to admit that they had been wrong.

Pray!

Do you find it hard to admit when you're wrong? Ask God to help you overcome that pride. And to react better when people criticise you.

How to grow a church

**Acts
11 v 19-26**

*I hate
gardening.*

*If I plant a seed,
it never seems
to grow.*

*I don't work
hard enough to
help the plant
grow.*

WEIRD WORDS

Persecution
Treated badly for
being Christians

Grace of God
God had been
so good to these
people, and He
changed their lives

Saul
Started off hating
Jesus but then
became a Christian!
He travelled around
telling people
about Jesus. Later
changed his name
to Paul.

You might have heard people talk
about **church planting**. They don't
mean a new church building has
grown out of the soil!

A church is a **group of Christians**
who worship God together. So
planting a church means a group of
believers starting to meet and serve
God together in a new place.

In today's Bible bit, a church is
planted in Antioch, a major city in
the Roman empire.

Read Acts 11 v 19-21

Just like a seed needs rain and
sunshine, churches need things to
help them grow.

Look out for 3 things a church
needs to grow as you...

Read verses 21-26

> **1. The most important one:**
>
> The _____
>
> **was with them (v21)**

> **2. They were encouraged to
> follow the Lord with all their
> h_____ (v23)**

> **3. Barnabas and Saul
> t_____ many
> people (v26)**

Pray!

Pray for your church or youth
group. Ask God for...
1. His blessing and help
2. Encouragement to keep going
3. Good Bible teaching

Check out verse 26 again
They were called Christians because
they **belonged to Christ**. They
were part of His family.

If you let your family down, it makes
them look bad.

Think!

Think how carefully Christians
need to behave, so they're not a
disgrace to Jesus Christ.
Are you a Christian? On spare
paper, write down how you can
be a better advert for Christ and
joining His family.

Giving for God

**Acts
11 v 27-30**

The growing group of believers in Acts are known as Christians.

That means belonging to Jesus Christ.

Today we'll see one way these people lived up to the name Christian.

WEIRD WORDS

Prophets
God's messengers

The brothers and sisters
Christians

Elders
Church leaders

Read Acts 11 v 27-28

Weird Bible bit

God's Holy Spirit helped this guy Agabus to predict a serious famine. Not so that he could show off. But to encourage the believers to help those in need.

Read verses 29-30

Belonging to Jesus Christ doesn't mean going to the right meetings and reading your Bible a bit. It involves your **whole** life.

These Christians showed their love for Jesus by **sending food and money to help other believers who were in need.**

We often hear of Christians driving trucks full of food, clothes and medicine into countries where disasters have happened.

It's a small way Christians can show concern for others who are facing tough times.

Action!

What are some ways YOU can help other Christians?

Pocket money to missionaries…

Shopping for elderly person…

_____

_____

_____

_____

_____

Ask God to help you get involved and do these things for Him.

Did you notice that these Christians gave **"as each one was able"** (v29)? That means as much as they could afford. Some had more money and possessions than others.

God knows how much we can afford. And how generous we've really been.

Wow!

Read Matthew 25 v 40
If you help others out of love for Jesus, it's just like doing it for Jesus Himself!

52

Prison break

**Acts
12 v 1-10**

We've been reading about the very first Christians and how they told many people about Jesus.

But they would soon have to suffer for it.

WEIRD WORDS

Festival of Unleavened Bread
A week-long festival just before Passover

Passover
Feast to remember God rescuing His people

Earnestly
Seriously

Read Acts 12 v 1-4

That's horrific! King Herod persecuted many Christians: throwing some in prison and killing others. James, one of Jesus' 12 disciples, was killed for telling people about Jesus. Peter was arrested too.

Pray!

Spend time praying for Christians around the world who are persecuted for telling people the amazing news that Jesus died for them.

Read verse 5

Things were looking bad for Peter, so what did loads of Christians do? Go back one letter.

‾ ‾ ‾ ‾ ‾ ‾ ‾ ‾

F B S O F T U M Z

‾ ‾ ‾ ‾ ‾ ‾

Q S B Z F E

‾ ‾ ‾   ‾ ‾ ‾

G P S   I J N

Wow!

That means praying again and again. When a situation seems bad, keep talking to God about it! He won't always answer in the way we expect, but He will answer!

Read verses 6-10 *to see what happened. Number the events in the order they occurred.*

○ Peter's chains fell off

○ Peter followed the angel out of prison

① Peter was asleep, chained between two soldiers

○ They walked down the street and the angel left him

○ The angel told Peter to get dressed and follow him

○ He thought he was seeing a vision!

○ An angel appeared and woke Peter up

Pray!

Who do you know that really needs God's help right now? Talk to God about them — ask Him to help. And keep asking!

53

Peter's prayer pointers

Peter was thrown into prison by Herod.

Peter's friends prayed for him and God sent an angel who rescued Peter!

(All of today's answers can be found using the code.)

Read Acts 12 v 11

What did Peter realise?

Prayer Pointer 1

Peter knew God had rescued him. When you pray, look for an answer! Make sure you **NOTICE** when God answers your prayers. And thank Him for it!

Read verses 12-15

When Rhoda told everyone that Peter was there, what did they say (v15)?

Prayer Pointer 2

They had prayed for Peter to be rescued from prison, but maybe they didn't **EXPECT** God to actually do it! When you pray, do you **EXPECT** and trust God to answer your prayers?

Read verses 16-17

What did Peter do?

Prayer Pointer 3

Peter told them how God had answered their prayers. When God answers your prayers, tell everyone!

Pray!

Talk to God right now. Which of the prayer pointers do you need to ask Him to help you with?

A	B	C	D	E	F	G	H	I	L	M	N	O	R	S	T	U	V	W	Y

Herod v God

54

**Acts
12 v 18-25**

*God rescued
Peter from
prison.*

*King Herod was
furious when he
found out...*

WEIRD WORDS

**No small
commotion**
A polite way
of saying: they
panicked, big style!

**Securing the
support**
Getting help from

Flourish
Grow, multiply

Read Acts 12 v 18-19

> *What did Herod do to the guards
> who didn't stop Peter escaping?*

Read verses 20-22

Important people from the cities of
Tyre and Sidon went to see Herod
and seek peace with him.

> *When they saw Herod, what did
> they shout (v22)?*

They thought he was a god. And
Herod didn't deny it! He certainly
didn't praise God as he should have.
Herod was a very nasty piece of
work.

Herod facts

• **He hated God's people,
Christians**

• **He tried to wipe them out by
throwing them in prison and
executing them**

• **Herod did not give God the
praise God deserved**

• **Herod was against God**

Read verses 23-25

> *What did God do to Herod
> (v23)?*

> *What happened to God's Word,
> the good news about Jesus
> (v24)?*

Herod wanted to wipe out
Christians. Instead, God wiped
Herod out! And God's Word spread,
so that loads more people became
Christians!

Pray!

Thank God that nothing or no
one is more powerful than Him!
Thank Him that nothing can
stop the good news of Jesus
spreading!

55

Sorcerer silenced

WEIRD WORDS

Tetrarch
Local ruler

Fasting
Going without food to spend extra time praying

Proclaimed
Preached

Synagogues
Where people worshipped God together

Sorcerer
Like a magician

False prophet
He claimed what he said was from God, but it wasn't

Proconsul
Local Roman ruler

Deceit
Lying, deceiving

Perverting
Twisting

Peter wasn't the only Christian having an exciting time…

Read Acts 13 v 1-3

Who did God choose to do special work for Him (v2)?

B_____

and S_____

Read verses 4-5

First stop: Cyprus (find it in an atlas), where they preached about God.

Who was helping them (apart from John)?

H_____ S_____

Pray!

The Holy Spirit lives in the lives of all Christians, helping them to serve God. Will you ask God to help you talk to your friends about Jesus?

Read verses 6-8

What was the important proconsul called?

S_____ P_____

He wanted Paul (new name for Saul, v9) and Barnabas to tell him about God. But someone else didn't want him to hear about God…

Who?

E_____ the

S_____

Would the proconsul believe Paul and Barnabas' message? Or would Elymas succeed?

But the battle wasn't really between **men**. Someone else was on each side.

Read verses 9-12

Paul and Barnabas and the

H_____ S_____ (v9)

against

Elymas and the

d_____ (v10)

Sergius Paulus was blown away by such power from God! He immediately knew that Paul and Barnabas' message about God was true.

Action!

Maybe you're worried about friends who the devil seems to have turned against God. **KEEP PRAYING! THE BATTLE ISN'T LOST!** And if God plans to save them, in the end there is no contest. God always wins.

2000 years of love

**Acts
13 v 13-25**

*Barnabas and
Paul (Saul's
new name!)
are travelling
around telling
people about
Jesus.*

Read Acts 13 v 13-15

Paul had been invited to speak in the synagogue. It was a great opportunity to preach about Jesus to both Jews and Gentiles! But he started by reminding the people of Jewish history.

Paul wanted to show them how God had cared for the Jewish people (Israelites) for 2000 years, despite all their ungratefulness and sin.

Read verses 16-25

Finish the chart by filling in the verse numbers.

> v20   v18   Judges 2 v 12   v17   v28   v24   v23   Mark 6 v 27   v21   v19

GOD'S LOVE	THE UNGRATEFUL PEOPLE
He led them out of Egypt. Verse _____	They disobeyed God in the desert. Verse _____
He gave them their own land (Canaan). Verse _____	They worshipped Canaanite gods. J_____
He gave judges to rule them. Verse _____	They wanted a king to rule them, not God. Verse _____
He sent John the Baptist to warn them to repent of their sins because their promised Saviour was coming soon. Verse _____	Many of them didn't believe John's message about Jesus. Herod murdered John. M_____
He sent Jesus to save them from their sins. Verse _____	They killed Jesus. Verse _____

WEIRD WORDS

Pamphylia
Part of Turkey

**The Law and
the Prophets**
Old Testament

Exhortation
Encouragement

Conduct
They disobeyed
God

Saviour
Rescuer

John
John the Baptist
who prepared the
way for Jesus

Wow!

God has shown His love for you in many ways. Especially in giving you the chance to know Jesus and be rescued from the punishment for sin.

Think & pray!

Are you ungrateful too? Have you rejected Jesus? Or do you now love and serve Jesus? Tell Jesus how you really feel about Him.

57

Acts
13 v 26-37

Paul is talking about Jesus.

*He has **bad news** and **good news**. First the bad news...*

WEIRD WORDS

Children of Abraham
Jewish believers

God-fearing Gentiles
Non-Jewish believers

Condemning
Sending Him to His death

Sabbath
The day Jews went to the synagogue

Subject to decay
Body rots in the ground

Holy One
Jesus Christ

Fell asleep
Died

What a comeback!

Read Acts 13 v 26-29

and fill in the vowels (aeiou).

BAD NEWS!

1. People in J__r__s__l__m didn't r__c__gn__se that J__s__s was the Son of God, who had come to rescue them (v27)...

2. ... even though every S__bb__th they read what the pr__ph__ts had predicted about Jesus! (v27)

3. They asked P__l__te to __xec__t__ Jesus even though there was no evidence against Him (v28).

The people should have welcomed Jesus with open arms. They were always reading about the **Saviour** that God had promised would come and **save** them.

There were over 300 prophecies about Jesus. And now they had come true! So what did the people do to the Saviour they had been waiting for? They killed Him.

But there was **good new**s too...

Read verses 30-37

GOOD NEWS!

1. God r__ __sed Jesus from the d__ __d! (v30)

2. Many people who had tr__v__ll__d with Jesus saw Him alive (v31).

3. Everything God pr__mised about J__s__s came true (v32-33). God had promised to send His Son and He'd promised that Jesus would not decay in the grave but be raised back to life (v35-37). It all came true!

Pray!

God raised Jesus from the dead! Jesus is alive! Does this good news make you happy and thankful? Then tell God right now!!

Tomorrow we'll find out why God raised Jesus back to life.

58

Why did Jesus **rise?**

Acts
13 v 38-41

Yesterday Paul told us that God raised His Son Jesus from the dead. Brilliant!

But why was this good news?

Read Acts 13 v 38-39

It was good news because...

it showed that only Jesus could save them from their sinful ways.

The Jewish people had always thought that **keeping God's laws** *(law of Moses)* was the way to please God. But no one **could** keep them! We're far too sinful!

Having God's laws showed them how imperfect and **sinful** they were. It was a way of teaching them how much they needed a Saviour to forgive them. They needed **Jesus**.

That's what the verse in this puzzle is saying. Follow the spiral to work it out.

S O T H E L A
U S T O C H W
D T B E J U R A
A H F A I S I S
L G Y T S P
E B H I T U
O M O F L H T
L W E M T A C I
T G R A H N
A H C

S_ ___ ___
___ ___ __
_____ __
____ __ __
_____
____ __
____ __
_____
__ _____

Galatians 3 v 24

Has Jesus forgiven your sins? He has if you've trusted in His death in your place. Then you are **justified** by faith in Him (see weird words).

It's **JUST AS IF I'D** never sinned! Get it? Remember it!

But watch out.

Read verses 40-41

That means if they rejected Jesus, they would one day suffer God's everlasting punishment for their sin.

Action!

If your sins are not forgiven, you are in deep danger. Don't push away Jesus' forgiveness any longer. It is free to everyone who trusts Him.

For info on *HOW TO BECOME A CHRISTIAN*, email discover@thegoodbook.co.uk or check out www.thegoodbook.co.uk/contact-us to find our UK mailing address.

Joseph: Dreamer drama

**Genesis
42 v 1-17**

*Time to get back
to the exciting
story of Joseph.*

*Do you need
a reminder of
what's happened
so far?*

WEIRD WORDS

Jacob/Israel
The same person!
Father of Joseph and
his eleven brothers.

Canaan
Where Joseph's
family lived. It's
the land that God
promised to give
to His people, the
Israelites.

In custody
In prison

The story so far...
Joseph's brothers hated him because
he dreamed that they'd bow down
to him. So they sold him as a slave
and told their father that he'd been
killed by a wild animal. Joseph
became a slave in Egypt but was
thrown into prison for a crime he
didn't commit.

He was released when he told
Pharaoh what his strange dreams
meant – there would be 7 good
years in Egypt and then 7 years
of horrible famine. Pharaoh made
Joseph his second-in-command, and
in charge of all the food! Joseph
was successful because **God was
with Him**.

Now read Genesis 42 v 1-8
There was a famine in Canaan,
where Joseph's family lived. So
Jacob sent 10 of his sons to Egypt to
bring back food. They had to buy it
from their brother Joseph! But they
didn't recognise him.

What did Joseph's brothers do?

They b_____ d_____
with their f_____ to
the g_____ (v6)

Remember Joseph's dreams? Flick
back to **Genesis 37 v 5-8**.

What had Joseph dreamed?

And now his dream had come true!
His brothers really did bow down to
him! God's plans for Joseph were
working out!

Read Genesis 42 v 9-17
Joseph claimed his brothers were
enemy spies! He was testing them
to see if they'd changed. To see if
they felt guilty for what they'd done
to him. He was probably getting
revenge too. Not such a good idea.

Pray!

Lots of amazing things had
happened in Joseph's life. Some
bad, some good. But they were
all part of God's plans for Joseph.
Thank God that His plans are
perfect, and that He's in total
control!

Surprise spies?

**Genesis
42 v 18-38**

*Want a recap
of what Joseph
and his brothers
are up to?
Well, look back
at yesterday's
Discover!*

*All of today's
missing words
can be found
in the centre of
the page.*

WEIRD WORDS

Fear God
Respect, love and
obey God

Households
Families

Verified
Checked that they
are true

Provisions
Food

Read Genesis 42 v 18-22

Joseph was testing his b_____. He wanted to keep one of them in p_____ while the others took food back to their s_____ families. But Joseph said they must bring back their y_____ brother, Benjamin. The brothers thought that God was p_____ them for treating J_____ so badly.

Read verses 23-26

They didn't know that Joe could u_____ every word they said. He now knew they felt bad for selling him as a s_____. He even c_____. Then he gave them back all the s_____ they'd spent, by putting it back in their s_____.

Benjamin · punishing · brothers · Reuben · cried · donkey · returned · father · sacks · silver · God · hearts · Jacob · Simeon · Joseph · slave · night · prison · starving · understand · youngest

Read verses 27-35

When the brothers stopped for the n_____, one of them went to feed his d_____. He found that the silver had been r_____ to his sack. Their h_____ sank and they said "What has G_____ done to us?" When they got home to their f_____, they told him all that had happened.

Read verses 36-38

J_____ was really upset. He blamed his sons for the loss of both Joseph and S_____ who was in Joseph's prison. Jacob wouldn't let them take B_____ in case they lost him too. The eldest brother, R_____, promised that Benjamin would be safe, but Jacob didn't believe him.

Think!

It was a long time since Joseph's brothers had sold him, but they couldn't forget it. Guilt made them afraid of God and worried about being punished. Do you feel guilty? God can forgive you! Say sorry and ask Him to.

Oh brother!

Genesis
43 v 1-34

Simeon is stuck in Joseph's jail.

And now his brothers are running out of food again...

WEIRD WORDS

Solemnly
Very seriously

Balm
Healing oil

Myrrh
Beauty oil

Bereaved
He felt like his sons were dead

Prostrating
Bowing down on the ground

Gracious
Give you more than you deserve

Hebrews
Israelites, God's special people

Skim read Genesis 43 v 1-14

Jacob didn't want to let his youngest son Benjamin go but he really had no choice. If they didn't get more food, they would starve to death. Plus they had to go back for Simeon.

What two things did Jacob say about God? (v14)

God is A_____y

God is so powerful. Nothing is bigger or stronger than God. He is in control of everything!

God shows m_____y

God often shows people great kindness when they deserve punishment. Jacob prayed that God would make things go well for his sons.

Read verses 15-25

Joseph invited his brothers round for dinner. They thought they'd be accused of stealing money. So they explained everything to the steward. *What did he say? (v23)*

> Don't be a_____.
> Your G_____ has given
> you treasure.

Even this Egyptian recognised that God was involved! It's great when people realise that God is involved in our lives.

Read verses 26-34

Joseph cried when he saw Benjamin. And he treated all his brothers really kindly. He clearly loved them all.

Think!

Write down the names of your brothers and sisters. (If you don't have any, use Christian friends instead — they're your brothers and sisters too!)

_____

_____

_____

Do you show them love? Do you treat them well?

_____

_____

Pray!

Ask God to help you show love to your brothers/sisters. And to show kindness to your Christian brothers and sisters. Now try and do it this week!

Getting the sack

62

Joseph is testing his brothers to see if they've changed their cruel ways.

Check out the crafty trick he pulls on them.

WEIRD WORDS

Steward
Chief servant

Divination
Using evil magic to make decisions. Joseph wasn't really using divination. It was a lie.

Tore their clothes
It was a sign of how incredibly upset they were.

Use the backwards words to fill in today's gaps.

rehtaf   deined   puc
s'nimajneB   nelots   haduJ
drawets   hpesoJ   sevals
skcas   dewob   eid   doof

Read Genesis 44 v 1-5

Joseph told his s_____ to fill his brothers' sacks with f_____ and to put their money back in their s_____ too. Also, to put Joseph's silver c_____ in Benjamin's sack. After they had left, J_____ sent his steward to catch them and accuse them of stealing.

Read verses 6-10

When the steward accused them, the brothers d_____ that they had s_____ the cup. They said that if any of them had the cup, he should d_____, and the rest would become s_____.

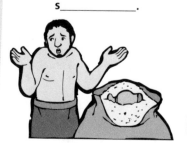

Read verses 11-17

Each of them opened their sacks and the cup was found in B_____. They all returned to Joseph and b_____ to him again! J_____ said that they were now all Joseph's slaves. But Joseph only wanted to keep Benjamin. He sent the rest back to their f_____.

Joseph was testing his brothers to see if they'd changed from their old ways. Had they?

YES/NO _____

Think!

How about you? Have you changed from your old sinful ways? Do you still live only for yourself? Or do you now want to live God's way?

_____

_____

_____

Pray!

Talk to God about your answer. Ask Him to help you change so that you become more and more like Him.

Judah and Jesus

**Genesis
44 v 18-34**

*So, the stolen
silver cup has
been found in
Benjamin's sack.*

*Now he's in
serious trouble.*

*Judah tries to get
Benjamin out of
trouble...*

Before

20 years earlier, Judah and his
brothers had sold Joseph as a slave
and told their father that Joseph
was dead! It had been Judah's idea
to get rid of Joseph.

**Now
Skim read Genesis 44 v 18-29**

Judah was now pleading with
Joseph to set Benjamin free. He
knew that if they went home
without him, their father Jacob
would die. So Judah did a
surprising thing...

Read verses 30-34

Complete what Judah said (v33).

> **Let me stay here as
> your s_____, instead
> of the b_____. Let him
> go back with his
> b_____.**

Wow! Judah really **had** changed.
He offered to take the punishment
in Benjamin's place. Nearly 2000
years later, Jesus would be born into
Judah's family. He would be King of
everything (that's what Genesis 49 v
10 is all about).

Like Judah, Jesus took the
punishment in someone else's place.
How did He do that?

_____

_____

_____

_____

(If you're not sure, check out
1 Peter 3 v 18)

Pray!

Thank God for sending Jesus to
take the punishment for your sin,
so that you can be forgiven!

Think!

Jesus has taken the punishment
you deserve for the wrong things
you've done. If you've trusted
Him to rescue you from that
punishment, then you're one of
Jesus' friends — a Christian! If
you haven't, maybe you need to...

Revealing the truth

Genesis 45 v 1-8

Lots of strange things have happened to Joseph, both good and bad.

WEIRD WORDS

Attendants
Servants

No ploughing and reaping
Because of the famine, no food could be grown.

Preserve for you a remnant
Joseph's family were rescued and would become God's great nation, the Israelites!

Deliverance
Rescue

Joseph's life
• sold by his brothers
• given a great job
• thrown into prison
• told Pharaoh what his dreams meant
• made second-in-command of Egypt

But Joseph's brothers still don't recognise him, so it's time for him to reveal his true identity.

Read Genesis 45 v 1-4
How did Joseph's brothers react to his news? (v3)

They were

t_____

Not surprising really! They thought Joseph was dead!

He must have seemed like a ghost to them. And now he had the power to get revenge on his brothers if he wanted to.

Read verses 5-8
and fill in the missing letters.

> **Don't feel bad about**
>
> **selli__g me as a slave!**
>   8
>
> **Go__ sent me to Egy__t to**
>   3   5
>
> **s__ve lives. It wasn't you who**
> 7
>
> **__ent me here, but G__d.**
> 4   2
>
> **God made made me the**
>
> **ru__er of all E__ypt.**
>   6   1

Now take the letters you filled in and put them in the same order as the numbers under them.

It was all part of

_ _ _ _ , _ _ _ _
1 2 3 4   5 6 7 8

All of the ups and downs in Joseph's life were a part of God's plan to rescue His people from the terrible famine.

Pray!

"In all things God works for the good of those who love him." (Romans 8 v 28)

If you're a Christian, God is using the ups and downs in your life for your good! Thank Him right now!

65

Unbelievable!

All of today's answers can be found in the wordsearch.

WEIRD WORDS

Goshen
Area of Egypt which is great for growing crops

Destitute
Very poor

Honour accorded me
How respected Joseph was

Fat of the land
All the best things in Egypt

Provisions
Food

300 shekels
3.5 kg of silver. That's loads!

```
B A C P H A R A O H B
E R C H O S K C J U V
L J O S E P H L A N D
I T N T R L X O L W I
E N V M H B J T I G E
V G I S O E G H V P D
E O N Y F S R E E R L
V S C F V T S S R U Q
N H E G Y P T W E L K
C E D B U D Y T X E P
A N M Q F A T H E R Z
```

Read Genesis 45 v 9-15

Joseph told his b_____ to go back to their f_____ and tell him that Joseph was now r_____ of Egypt. And they should bring him and their whole family back to E_____. They could live in G_____ which was a great place for farming.

Read verses 16-24

P_____ was delighted to hear that Joseph's brothers were moving to Egypt. He promised to give them the best l_____. And they didn't need to bring any belongings because they could have the b_____ things in Egypt. Joseph also gave them loads of stuff, including new c_____.

Think!

How generous are YOU?

What do you have that you could give to someone who needs it more?

_____

_____

_____

_____

Read verses 25-28

When they got back to their father Jacob, they said: "Joseph is a_____! At first, he didn't b_____ them. But when they showed him all the things that J_____ had sent him, he was c_____ that he would see Joseph before he d_____!

Do you take your family for granted? Or do you thank God for the home and family He's given you? Think of some of the good things about your family.

Pray!

Ask God to help you to be more generous. And thank Him for some of the things you like about your family.

Change of plan?

Genesis
46 v 1-7

In the past,
God had made
loads of great
promises to
Jacob's family
(the Israelites).

One of them
was that God
would give
them the land
of Canaan to
live in.

WEIRD WORDS

Israel
Jacob

Sacrifices
Gifts to God

Livestock
Animals, like sheep,
donkeys, camels
etc.

Offspring
Children and
grandchildren

> So how come they're
> now all moving out of Canaan
> and into Egypt. Surely this can't
> be part of God's plans?

Read Genesis 46 v 1-4

God spoke to Jacob in a vision,
saying it was OK to go to Egypt. He
also made four more promises to
Jacob. *To discover them, go back
one letter each time.*

1. I will make you into a

_ _ _ _ _
H S F B U

_ _ _ _ _ _
O B U J P O

God had already promised that
Jacob's family would grow into a
huge nation. Now He's saying that
this will happen while they're all
in Egypt.

2. _ _ _ _ _ _ _
J X J M M H P

_ _ _ _ _ _
X J U I Z P V

God promised to be with Jacob and
the Israelites in Egypt.

3. _ _ _ _ _ _
J X J M M

_ _ _ _ _
C S J O H

_ _ _ _ _ _
Z P V C B D L

God would bring the Israelites back
to Canaan. Years earlier, God had
told Jacob's grandad (Abraham) that
his family would be slaves in Egypt,
and then God would take them all
back to Canaan. It's in **Genesis 15 v
13-16** if you want to check.

4. _ _ _ _ _ _ **will**
K P T F Q I
be with you when you die

Jacob had thought he would never
see Joseph again. He could hardly
believe it!

Read verses 5-7

Jacob and his whole family went
to live with Joseph in Egypt.
(Verses 8-27 tell us exactly who
they all were.)

Pray!

Thank God that He is so good
to His people, and always
keeps His brilliant promises to
them!

67

Genesis 46 & 47

Jacob's just found out that his son Joseph is still alive!

So he sets off for Egypt with the whole family...

WEIRD WORDS

Tend livestock
Look after animals such as sheep and cows

Detestable
Disgusting

Pilgrimage
A journey to somewhere you really want to go. Here it means Jacob's life.

Jacob's journey

Read Genesis 46 v 26-34

Together again

Jacob is finally reunited with the son he thought was dead. It's a touching moment. Jacob says he can now die a happy man.

Clever plan

Joseph asks his brothers to tell Pharaoh that they are shepherds. Bizarrely, Egyptians hate shepherds! So maybe Pharaoh will send them to Goshen where they can live safely, separate from the Egyptians. Nice plan.

Read Genesis 47 v 1-6

Even better!

The plan worked. Pharaoh let Joseph's family live in Goshen — the best place in Egypt!

He even offered some of them really good jobs (v6). God was looking after His people.

Read verses 7-12

Nice one, Joseph!

Jacob and Pharaoh seemed to get on well. And when his family settled in Goshen, Joseph looked after them and gave them plenty of food.

How did Jacob describe his life? (first part of v9)

_____

_____

Some Bible versions say *pilgrimage*, or *years of wandering*. Jacob saw his life with God as a long **journey**.

Our lives are like a journey too...

You start by going wherever YOU want to go.

If you become a Christian then you start travelling where GOD wants you to go.

Sometimes you'll find obstacles that stop you going God's way. Or people will persuade you to go their way instead of God's.

But God always gives us the chance to go back to His way, living for Him.

Pray!

How's your journey with God going? Ask Him to help you to go His way, so that you serve Him with your life.

No food = no fun

**Genesis
47 v 13-31**

*Joseph's family
moved to Egypt.*

*But then the
famine kicked in.*

WEIRD WORDS

In bondage
In slavery

Desolate
Empty of life

Servitude
Slavery

**Allowance /
Allotment**
Amount of food

Fruitful
Had lots of kids!

Faithfulness
Loyalty

Read Genesis 47 v 13-22

The famine hit Egypt really hard. The people ran out of food and went to Joseph to buy it from his huge stores. When they ran out of money, they paid for it with their animals, or their land. When they had nothing left, they sold themselves as slaves to Pharaoh.

Read verses 23-27

Joseph was wise. He gave the people seeds so they could grow their own crops. But he made them give a fifth of everything they grew to Pharaoh. The people seemed happy with this deal.

Things seemed a lot easier for Joseph's family. Fill in the vowels to show what happened.

The __sr__ __l__t__s lived in G__sh__n, where they bought pr__p__rty, were fr__ __tf__l and increased in n__mb__rs. That means they had lots of ch__ldr__n!

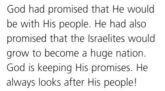

Wow!

God had promised that He would be with His people. He had also promised that the Israelites would grow to become a huge nation. God is keeping His promises. He always looks after His people!

Read verses 28-31

Jacob made his son Joseph promise to treat him and his family well. The hand under the thigh sealed the promise.

Complete two great facts about Jacob (they're in v30-31).

FACT 1

**Jacob asked J__s__ph to
b__ry him outside of __gypt.**

He wanted to be buried in Canaan, the land God had promised to the Israelites. He wanted to be in God's country.

FACT 2

**J__c__b (also called Israel)
w__rsh__pp__d G__d**

He may have been old and frail, but it didn't stop him from worshipping God. So what's your excuse?

Pray!

Spend time worshipping God right now. Praise Him for how great He is. Thank Him for what He's done in your life. And ask Him to help you worship Him by living in a way that pleases Him.

Feeling **sheep**ish?

Jacob is at the end of his life.

But he's not sad, because he knows how brilliant God has been to him in his life.

Read Genesis 48 v 1-4

Jacob remembered 2 of the great promises God had made to him.

Fill in the first letter of each word to complete the promises.

1. I __ill __ncrease __our __umbers (v4)

God had promised that Jacob's family (the Israelites) would grow and grow. It was already happening!

2. I __ill __ive __ou __his __and __or ever (v4)

Jacob trusted that God would give the country of Canaan to his family and one day they would all live there.

Because God had been so good to him in the **past**, Jacob knew that God would keep His promises in the **future**.

Next, Jacob adopted Joseph's sons Ephraim and Manasseh (it's in verses 5-10).

Now read verses 11-16

Jacob blessed Ephraim and Manasseh and accepted them as part of his family. *What great fact does Jacob tell us about God (v15)?*

__od __as __een __y
__hepherd __ll __y __ife

God had always been with Jacob, looking after him, keeping him in line, and showing him the way to live.

Wow!

God is a shepherd to all His people (Christians). He's always with them and He shows them the right way to live. He is always looking after them!

Read verses 17-22

You're supposed to bless the eldest son, and they'll become the head of the family one day. But Jacob blessed Ephraim, who was younger than Manasseh. It was all part of God's plan for the Israelites.

What else did Jacob say? (v21)

__od __ill __e
__ith __ou (v21)

Jacob knew that God would always be with Joseph. And God is always with His people!

Pray!

Thank God that He looks after His people, leads them and is always with them!

Roar data

Genesis
49 v 1-12

Before he died, Jacob gathered all his sons together to bless them.

WEIRD WORDS

Firstborn
Eldest son

Excelling in
Having lots of

Turbulent
Causing trouble

Defiled it
Made it impure

Hamstrung
Crippled

Rouse him
Wake him up

Sceptre / ruler's staff
A king's golden pole. A symbol of power.

Everything he said about his sons would come true...

Reuben
Read Genesis 49 v 1-4

Reuben was the eldest son, so he expected to inherit loads and become head of the family. But Reuben turned against Jacob, so he would no longer get all these things.

Simeon and Levi
Read verses 5-7

Jacob cursed Simeon and Levi because they had murdered lots of people. He said that their families would be scattered all over the place. Years later, this came true.

Judah's blessing is a bit long and confusing. So unjumble the anagrams and read the explanations.

Judah
Read verses 8-12

Your brothers will

p_____ you (v8)
i s p e a r

Judah's family would become the most important tribe.

You are like a l_____ (v9)
n o i l

Lions are brave, strong and king of the animals. Judah and his family would be like that!

The s_____
t c r e e p s
will not leave Judah until
the one it b_____ to
l e n s g o b
comes. He will have the
o_____
e d o b e n i c e
of nations (v10).

This is the important bit! Someone from Judah's family will be King and all the nations will obey Him! And life will be brilliant (v11-12).

Wow!

This came true too. Jesus was born into Judah's family. He is the King in control of everything. And when He comes back, *everyone* will obey Him!

Pray!

Spend time praising Jesus for how great He is! He is the King in control of everything!

Genesis 49 v 13-28

Benjamin

Zebulun

...e Almighty

Name game

Asher

Mighty One

Issachar

Gad

Dan

Read Genesis 49 v 13-18

Jacob is blessing his sons one by one. *Fill in their names. They're all hidden around the page.*

Z_____ and his family would live near the sea.

I_____ would be strong but lazy (like a donkey).

D_____ and his family would fight for the Israelites. But they'd mess up sometimes too. Samson came from Dan's tribe. He fought for Israel but he messed up too.

In verse 18, Jacob quickly prays, asking God to rescue his family.

Shepherd

Read verses 19-21 and 27-28

G_____ and his family will often battle with robbers.

A_____ and his tribe will grow great food!

Joseph

N_____ is like a deer that runs free. I've no idea what that means! (If you do, let me know!)

B_____ is like a hungry wolf. His tribe would be aggressive and violent. King Saul was from his tribe.

Read verses 22-26

J_____

His blessing is great! Joseph suffered a lot in his life, but things worked out because God was always with him, looking after him. Joseph's family would gain all the great blessing that God had promised Jacob. Fantastic!

Find some of the names for God that Jacob uses (v24-25).

M_____ O_____

S_____

R_____ of I_____

The A_____

Rock of Israel

Pray!

All these names are used to describe how great, powerful and loving God is. Spend time praising our awesome God right now.

Naphtali

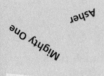

WEIRD WORDS

Haven
Safe place

Burden
Heavy thing that needs carrying

Submit to forced labour
Become a slave

Deliverance
Rescue

Delicacies
Tasty things

Doe and fawns
Deer

Ravenous
Really hungry!

Plunder
Treasure

Hostility
Hatred

Bounty
Treasure

Good mourning

WEIRD WORDS

Gathered to my people
Go to heaven

Ephron the Hittite
Man who Abraham bought land from

Physicians
Doctors

Embalm
Preserve the body so it doesn't decay

Mourned
Showed sadness

Dignitaries
Important people

Threshing-floor
Where grain was sorted

Lamented
Cried out

Jacob was over 140 when he died!

Read Genesis 49 v 29-33

God had promised to give Jacob's family the country of Canaan. That's why Jacob wanted to be buried there. He knew that God would one day keep His promise.

> I am about to be gathered to my people

That's how Jacob described his death. **His people** means his dad Isaac and his grandad Abraham. And other people like them who loved and trusted God.

Wow!

Jacob knew that dying wasn't the end for him! He knew that he would go to be with God in heaven! And that he'd be there with other people who loved God!

Read Genesis 50 v 1-14

and cross out the wrong words.

Joseph was very happy/ upset when his father died. The people mourned for 50/60/70 days. Joseph went to bury Jacob in Cambridge/ Canaan/Canada. Loads of important people from Egypt/England went with him, as did all his sisters/ brothers/brussel sprouts. There were also loads of horsemen and chariots/carrots.

What a huge funeral!

Think!

Do you worry about dying?

YES/NO _____

Or about someone you know dying?

YES/NO _____

If we love and trust Jesus, we don't need to be scared of dying! We know that we will be with Him in eternal life for ever!

Pray!

How does that make you feel? Talk to God and tell Him. You can be totally honest about your thoughts and feelings.

Unforgettable

73

Genesis 50 v 15-21

It's your mum's birthday.

The problem is...

you've forgotten to get her a present!

Panic!

Why is it so easy to forget things we really need to remember?!

Yet it seems **impossible** to forget things which you'd rather not think about again. Stuff you'd like to forget.

Especially **wrong stuff**, like the time you really upset your friend, or did something you shouldn't have.

It hurts to remember these things. But it's good to feel sorry and ashamed sometimes. It helps us to avoid doing it again.

Joseph's brothers still remembered how badly they'd treated Joseph years ago.

Read Genesis 50 v 15-18

They were right to feel ashamed. But they were wrong to lie to get Joseph to forgive them. *What did they think Joseph would do to them? Circle your answers.*

be angry with them

punish them

forgive them

show his love for them

But they were wrong...

Read verses 19-21

Joseph had already forgiven them. *What did he say?*

> Don't be a_____.
> You intended to h_____
> me but God intended it
> for g_____, so that
> many l_____ could be
> saved! Don't worry, I will
> take care of you and your
> c_____.

That's amazing! Joseph's brothers expected him to punish them. Instead, he forgave them. And he gave them loads too.

Wow!

That's what Jesus is like with us if we're sorry for the wrong things we've done and ask Him to forgive us.

We deserve to be punished, but instead He FORGIVES us. He saves our lives from the punishment we deserve. And He looks after us, giving us far more than we deserve!

Pray!

Got anything you want to say to Jesus? Go on then...

Bye Bye Joseph

**Genesis
50 v 22-26**

*Today we reach
the end of
Joseph's story.*

*And it's the end
of Genesis too.*

*It's an
emotional
moment.*

WEIRD WORDS

**Third
generation**
Great-
grandchildren

Embalmed
Treated the body so
it didn't decay

Joseph: This Is Your Life

- Joseph was his father's favourite son.

- But his brothers hated him and sold him as a slave.

- He was thrown into jail for a crime he didn't commit.

- But Joseph was successful, even in prison!

- He interpreted Pharaoh's dreams and Pharaoh made him second-in-command of Egypt.

- Joseph's brothers bowed down to him, and Joseph forgave them for the past.

*Why did things work out for
Joseph? Go back one letter to find
out (B=A, C=D, E=D etc).*

```
__ __ __   __ __ __ __
U  I  F    M  P  S  E

__ __ __   __ __ __ __
X  B  T    X  J  U  I

__ __ __ __ __ __
K  P  T  F  Q  I
```

(Genesis 39 v 2)

Now read Genesis 50 v 22-26

*What did Joseph believe God would
do (v24)?*

God will take care of you and

```
__ __ __ __   __ __ __
U  B  L  F    Z  P  V

__ __   __ __ __   __ __
V  Q    P  V  U    P  G

__ __ __ __   __ __ __ __
U  I  J  T    M  B  O  E
```

Joseph knew that God would
continue to look after his family.
And one day God would lead
them to Canaan, the land He had
promised to give them. Joseph
asked for his bones to be carried out
of Egypt when they left!

Wow!

400 years later, both promises
were kept. God led Moses and the
Israelites out of Egypt and eventually
into Canaan. And Joseph's bones
were taken with them! (Exodus 13
v 18-19)

Pray!

Thank God that He's totally trust-
able. Ask Him to help you to trust
Him more and more.

To see how Genesis fits into the story
of the Bible, ask for the free e-booklet
LITTLE BOOK, BIG PICTURE. Email
discover@thegoodbook.co.uk
or check out
www.thegoodbook.co.uk/contact-us
to find our UK mailing address.

Colossians: Just Jesus

**Colossians
1 v 1-2**

A couple of weeks ago we were reading Acts. (Flick back to days 44 – 58 if you can't remember!) Paul was spreading the good news of Jesus.

Today we start reading Colossians — Paul's letter to a group of new Christians.

WEIRD WORDS

Grace
Grace is God sending Jesus to rescue people from their sins, even though they deserve to be punished for disobeying God.

Colossians – the lowdown

Who's the letter to?
A group of young Christians in Colossae in Turkey.

What's the problem?
These Christians were being led away from Jesus by ungodly preachers.

What's the solution?
Paul reminds them of some amazing truths about Jesus. And he tells them what it means to live as a Christian.

What about us?
Well, don't you need to know those things too?

Let's get started!

Read Colossians 1 v 1
Paul starts off by reminding the Colossians who he is.

> **An a_____ of
> C_____ J_____**

That means he's been sent out by God to tell people about Jesus.

Paul also sends greetings from Timothy, who travelled with him.

Read verse 2
What three things does Paul call these Colossians?

1. H_____
Set apart to serve God

2. F_____
They stuck to the truth about Jesus

**3. B_____ and
s_____ in
C_____**
Part of God's family, because Jesus had forgiven their sins

Pray!
If you're a Christian, these things should be true for you too. Ask God for these three things to be true in your life.

> **Paul wished g_____
> and p_____ to these
> Christians (v2).**

Think & pray!
When you pray for your friends and family, do you pray that they will receive God's grace (see Weird Words)? And that they'll have peace from knowing that God has forgiven their sins? Why not pray those things right now?

Heavenly hope

**Colossians
1 v 3-8**

*Paul is writing
to new
Christians in the
city of Colossae.*

WEIRD WORDS

Faith
Belief, trust

God's people
Christians

Bearing fruit
People becoming
Christians

God's grace
God sending Jesus
to rescue people
from sin, even
though they don't
deserve it

Spirit
All Christians have
the Holy Spirit
helping them to
serve God and love
others

*All of today's missing words can be
found in the word pool.*

> **Christ   effect   faith
> gospel   growing   heaven
> love   hope   love   fruit
> Spirit   thank   world**

Read Colossians 1 v 3-5

We t_____
God because of your
f_____ in C_____
Jesus and the l_____ you
have for all God's people
(v4). Your faith and love
spring from the h_____
you have stored up for
you in h_____ (v5)

The hope Paul talks about in verse 5
isn't an uncertain one. It's not like
hoping you maybe might possibly
get an iPhone for your birthday! It's
more like the certain hope you have
if you know you dad has already
bought you one.

Wow!

We know that if our faith is in
Jesus, eternal life will be full of good
things for us. So we should want to
live lives of faith and love for God,
just as He wants us to!

Read verses 5-8

Paul is talking about the **gospel**
— the amazing news that Jesus
Christ died on the cross to take the
punishment for all the wrongs we
have done. So if we trust in Him, we
can have all our sins forgiven!

**1. They can see its
e_____ all over the
w_____ (v6)**

The amazing truth about Jesus has
spread all over the world, changing
people's lives.

**2. The g_____ is
bearing f_____
and g_____ (v6)**

When people turn to Jesus their lives
are changed. They start to live for
God and not for themselves.

**3. Their lives show l_____
which comes from the
S_____ (v8)**

God's Holy Spirit helps us to show
love to others.

Pray!

Ask God to help you to bear fruit.
To serve Him and do good things
for Him. So that others can see
how your life has changed.

Will power

Read Colossians 1 v 9

Fit the letter blocks into the right places to show what Paul was praying for these Christians.

Paul says he wants the Colossians to know God's will for them — how God wants them to live. How about praying that for your friends?

Pray!

Dear Lord, help me to tell my friends about Your love for them. Let them know how You want them to live.

WEIRD WORDS

His will
How God wants you to live

Glorious might
Awesome power

Endurance
Sticking at living God's way

Inheritance of his holy people in the kingdom of light
All Christians (holy people) will go to live with God forever

Redemption
Jesus died to buy us back from sin. He paid the price for our sins. Christians now belong to Him.

So how does God want His people (Christians) to live?

Read verses 10-12

God wants Christians to live in a way that pleases Him. But how?

> **1. Bearing fruit (v10)**
> Serving God in the things you do
>
> **2. Strengthened by God (v11)**
> We need God's help
>
> **3. Showing endurance and patience (v11)**
> Putting up with any hassle we get for living God's way

Read verses 12-14

Sounds weird, but this is amazing stuff. Here's what it means...

Wow!

Christians are God's children. They will inherit eternal life with God. He has rescued them from sin (the dominion of darkness) so they can live with Him for ever!

Pray!

If you're a Christian, thank God for forgiving your sins and promising you His amazing inheritance — the gift of living for ever with Him!

God's great image

Next up,
Paul tells the
Colossians some
fantastic truths
about Jesus.

**Firstborn over
all creation**

In Bible times, the
oldest son (the
one who was
born first) had
special rights and
privileges. And so
does **Jesus** — He
is in charge of the
whole of creation!
Jesus rules!

Read Colossians 1 v 15-18

*From these verses find the **two
words** that complete all these great
truths about Jesus.*

_____

**were created through Him
and for Him (v16)**

**He is before
_____ (v17)**

**In Him _____
_____
hold together (v17)**

Do you get the point???

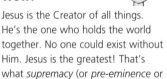

Wow!

Jesus is the Creator of all things.
He's the one who holds the world
together. No one could exist without
Him. Jesus is the greatest! That's
what *supremacy* (or *pre-eminence* or
first place) means in verse 18.

Recognise the woman at the top
right of the page? You've probably
seen Queen Elizabeth II on TV or in
a newspaper. Even though we might
never have met her, we recognise
the Queen's **image**.

God is far far more powerful
than the Queen! But how do
we know what He's like if we've
never seen Him?

Read verse 15 again

We can't see God, but Jesus is the
image of Him. We know what God
is like by learning about His Son,
Jesus.

Think!

Write down things you
know about Jesus. Include stuff
from today's verses.

_____

_____

_____

_____

Pray!

Praise and thank Jesus for this
glimpse of what God is like.
Ask Him to help you learn more
about Him.

Cross purposes

Paul is teaching us some amazing things about Jesus.

Time to recap on what Paul taught us yesterday.

Read Colossians 1 v 15-18 again, then verses 19-20

Lightly shade in the boxes that contain correct statements. The verses in each box will help you work out if the statements are true or false.

Jesus is nothing like God (v15)	Jesus shows us what God is like (v15)	The world doesn't need Jesus (v17)
The world needs Jesus to keep it going (v17)	Jesus is in charge of all His followers — the church (v18)	Jesus is the creator of all things (v16)
Jesus has nothing to do with the church (v18)	Jesus is fully God (v19)	Jesus didn't create the earth (v16)
Jesus isn't in control (v19)	Jesus' death (blood) can give us peace with God (v20)	Jesus' death leaves us as God's enemies (v20)

WEIRD WORDS

His fullness
Everything about God

Dwell
Live

Reconcile
Put things right with God. When Jesus died on the cross, He made it possible for us to be at peace with God.

If you got it right, you should be able to see a cross.

People were telling the Colossians they needed to do **more** than believe in Jesus and be forgiven by Him. But that's not true.

Wow!

Jesus is more than just a special human being. He is actually God. Yet He lived as a human so that He could die on the cross in our place. It was the only way to make it possible for us to be put right with God.

Pray!

Thank God that His Son's death is the only thing we need to put things right between God and us.

Before and after

Colossians 1 v 21-23

Ever seen adverts like the one on the right?

They show someone BEFORE and AFTER using a product.

WEIRD WORDS

Alienated
Separated

Reconciled
See yesterday's Weird Words

Holy
Perfect, set apart to serve God

Blemish
Fault, imperfection, sin

Gospel
The good news about Jesus

SUPERSLIM
WEIGHT LOSS PILLS

Before   **After**

Read Paul's before and after for Jesus...

Read Colossians 1 v 21-23

Verse 21 gives us the **before** and verse 22 gives the **after**.

Work your way through the maze to find out the difference Jesus makes.

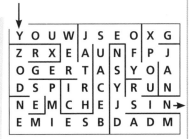

BEFORE

Y _ _   _ _ _ _
    _ _ _ _ _ ,
_ _ _ _ _ _ _ _
_ _ _ _ _ _ _ _ _
_ _   _ _ _ _
_ _ _

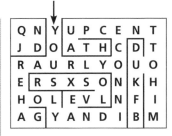

AFTER

Y_ _   _ _ _
_ _ _ _   _ _ _
_ _ _ _ _ _ _ _
_ _   _ _ _

What an incredible difference! This is the difference Jesus makes to Christians' lives.

Before
They were separated from God by their sins.
After
Christians are at peace with God. Their sins have been forgiven.

There's nothing **we** can do to bring about this change. It's all down to **Jesus** dying on the cross to take our punishment. If we turn to Him, He forgives us and makes us God's friends again.

Want to know *HOW TO BECOME GOD'S FRIEND – A CHRISTIAN?* Ask us for a free fact sheet. Email discover@thegoodbook.co.uk or check out www.thegoodbook.co.uk/contact-us to find our UK mailing address.

God's great mystery

**Colossians
1 v 24-29**

*Today's Bible bit is tricky to figure out. To solve **God's great mystery**, fill in the missing words after reading the verses.*

Clue 1: Read verse 24

Paul went through a lot of hassle for Jesus' followers, who we call the ch_____. We want to find out who Paul really suffered for.

Clue 2: Read verse 25

The answer to the mystery is something to do with fulfilling the w_____ of G_____ — God's promises coming true.

Clue 3: Read verse 26

The mystery has been h_____ for ages, but now has been made known to the L_____ people. That means Christians.

Clue 4: Read verse 27

Paul sums up the great mystery — C_____ in you, the hope of g_____

The answer!

Jesus Christ is the answer. Jesus fulfils God's word. He fulfils God's promise to rescue His people. Jesus is the answer to our problems. Jesus is God's message to us. He is our only way to forgiveness and everlasting life with God.

Read verses 28-29

God has revealed this great mystery to us — that trusting Jesus is the only way to have our sins forgiven. So, like Paul, we must **work hard** at sharing this mystery, so that more people turn to Jesus!

Still clueless?

So far we've learned that the mystery is something to do with God's promises coming true. It's something for the good of the church. It has been kept hidden for ages, but now is revealed to Christians.

You're close to solving it....

Pray!

Thank God that He has revealed the amazing message of Jesus to you. Ask Him to help you share it.

What a **treasure!**

**Colossians
2 v 1-7**

*False teachers
have been
telling the new
Christians in
Colossae all
sorts of rubbish.*

*So Paul is
setting them
straight on a
few things.*

WEIRD WORDS

Laodicea
City 11 miles from
Colossae

Disciplined
Organised

Read Colossians 2 v 1-5

Paul knew all about hard work
and tough times. We read about
it in Acts — murder attempts,
snake attack, false trials, prison, a
shipwreck!

But Paul didn't mind going through
hard times for the sake of these
Christians. He knew the hard work
was worth it, so they would be
strengthened and encouraged in
their faith in Jesus.

Read verses 2-3

Paul tells us that the treasures of
God are found in **Jesus**. So we
don't need anything else. Paul
wants the Colossians (and us) to
know this and not be persuaded
that they need anything else.

> *What other things do people say
> we need? Add your own.*
>
> **You need lots of money**
>
> **You need a boy/girlfriend**

Read verses 6-7

Paul is saying: you've started well
following Jesus — now stick at it!
Fill in the vowels please!

How you started

You received Chr__st

as L__rd

Paul talks about Jesus as Lord.
That means Jesus is in charge of a
Christian's life. Every part of it.

How you're
carrying on

Continue to l__v__ in Him.

B__ __ld your lives on him

and become str__ng__r

in your f__ __th.

Jesus gives Christians everything
they need. He saved them from their
sins. He's given them the Bible to
teach them, and the Holy Spirit to
help them live for Him!

*What else does Paul say we need to
be (v7)?*

Filled to overflowing with

t_____

Pray!

Jesus has done so much for you.
Take some extra time now to
THANK HIM for what He's done
in your life.

Hollow hopes

**Colossians
2 v 8-12**

Some drink bottles are designed to make it look like there's more drink in there than there really is. Annoying isn't it?

Paul warns us about people whose ideas about life are like that. They promise a lot, but really they're just hollow and empty.

Read Colossians 2 v 8
Go back one letter to complete the explanation.

Don't fall for

— — — — — — — —
U F B D I J O H

which relies on man-made rules instead of

— — — — — —
D I S J T U

Next, Paul reminds Christians about what they do believe...

Read verses 9-10

Jesus is

— — — — —   — — —
G V M M Z   H P E

**Through Jesus,
Christians are made**

— — — — — — — —.
D P N Q M F U F

We don't need anything else. Only _ _ _ _ _ **can**
K F T V T

save us from our sins.

Read verse 11

Don't worry, we don't need to be circumcised! Jesus

— — — — **in our place**
E J F E

so that we can be part of His family. We need to

— — — —   — — — —
U V S O   B X B Z

from our sinful ways to show that we're now on God's side.

Read verse 12

Baptism is getting dunked in water to show that you follow Jesus and have **turned away** from your old sinful ways.

Christians should _ _ _ _
C V S Z

(turn away from) their old way of life. They believe in

— — — ,   — — — — —
H P E T   Q P X F S

which has raised them to a new life with Jesus.

Pray!

Nailing the **truth**

**Colossians
2 v 13-15**

*Some more
tricky verses
today!*

*But stick with
it, because
Paul's got some
awesome things
to tell us about
God.*

WEIRD WORDS

Uncircumcision
Not belonging to
God, disobeying
Him

Indebtedness
Owing payment

Condemned
Said we are guilty

**Disarmed the
powers and
authorities**
Conquered evil

---

*Use the word pool to fill in all
the gaps.*

> authorities   pay   dead
>
> sins   cancelled   alive
>
> powers   cross

Read Colossians 2 v 13

> **When you were _____
> in your _____, God
> made you _____
> with Christ.**

These people were as good as dead
— they were separated from God by
their sins against Him. But now God
had made them alive. He'd forgiven
their sins and brought them back
to Him.

These guys had disobeyed God and
there was nothing **they** could do to
put things right with Him.

It's like owing someone a billion
dollars. A debt you could never pay
off by yourself. But...

Read verse 14

> **God _____
> the *charge* of our *legal
> indebtedness*. That means
> He totally wiped out the
> debt which these guys
> couldn't _____.
> Jesus died on
> the _____ to pay
> the debt for them.**

We could never live a life good
enough to satisfy God's high
standards. But He wipes out the sin
of those who turn to Him!

Read verse 15

> **God defeated the
> _____ and
> _____**

When Jesus was raised back to life,
God publicly defeated death, sin and
the evil powers (like the devil) that
are against Him and His people!

Read through the boxes again. God
has done all this for **you**!

Pray!

*Thank you Lord, for sending your
Son Jesus to die on the cross and
pay for my sins. Thank you for
raising Him to life to beat death
and sin for ever!*

Chasing shadows

Colossians
2 v 16-23

> Jo's dad went to work in another country for a few months. All Jo had to remind her of him was a photograph. But when her dad came back, Jo didn't keep looking at the photo, because she had her dad back. Why waste time with a picture when you can have the real thing?

WEIRD WORDS

False humility
Pretending to put others first

Disqualify you
Keep you from heaven

Idle notions
Selfish ideas

The Head
Jesus

Ligaments / sinews
Stuff connecting parts of the body

Elemental spiritual forces
Ungodly ideas

Destined to perish
Bound to fail

Self-imposed
Created by false teachers

Sensual indulgence
Desire to sin

Read Colossians 2 v 16-17

These people said that you must follow loads of rules to be right with God.
Paul says that these rules are only s_____.
The reality is found in C_____ (v17).

These Old Testament rules pointed towards Jesus coming to save His people. Now Jesus is here, He's the only way to be forgiven. Keeping these rules just isn't enough.

Now read verses 18-23

Don't be fooled by what people say. Stick with Jesus and you can't go wrong. He is the Head — He's in charge of our lives. If we stay close to Him, we will grow as Christians. We only get the full Christian life if we look to **Jesus** (not other people) to provide it.

Think!

What things might people mistakenly follow instead of Jesus for a full Christian life? Add your own ideas.

Worshipping God in a certain way

Having certain spiritual gifts

_____

_____

_____

_____

These things may not be bad. But if people say you must do these things to be a Christian... **DON'T LISTEN TO THEM!**

Wow!

Trying to keep rules won't put you right with God. Only trusting in Jesus to forgive you leads to a full Christian life.

What are you looking at?

**Colossians
3 v 1-4**

*Now Paul
moves on to
how to live as a
Christian.*

*Paul tells us
what has
happened to
Christians in the
PAST, what's
true for them
in the PRESENT,
and what will
happen in the
FUTURE.*

Read Colossians 3 v 1-4

*Use the wordsearch to fill in all of
today's spaces.*

H	A	S	C	P	C	F	L
G	Z	F	H	J	L	G	Q
O	E	A	R	T	H	L	Y
D	X	D	I	C	I	O	V
R	A	I	S	E	D	R	A
D	N	E	T	U	D	Y	O
B	T	D	B	G	E	R	K
Y	E	S	M	I	N	D	S
A	P	P	E	A	R	S	D

The Past

**Christians have d_____
(v3) and been r_____
with C_____ (v1).**

Christians have died to their old
sinful way of living. And they have
been **raised** with Jesus to live for
Him and with Him.

The Present

**Christians' lives are now
h_____ with Christ
in G_____ (v3).**

Because Jesus died for them,
Christians are joined with Him. Their
lives are **hidden** with Him (and God
the Father) in heaven. That means
their future with God is safe.

The future

**A Christian's new life
is in Christ. When Jesus
a_____ again,
Christians will appear with
Him in g_____ (v4).**

When Jesus comes back to judge
the world, Christians will be revealed
to be God's children. They will
become like Jesus!

Read through the past, present and
future bits again. So what should
Christians be doing now?

**Set your m_____
on things above, not on
e_____ things (v2).**

Christians must put their old sinful
lives behind them. And live their
lives for God, remembering that
they will live with Him for ever as
His children.

Pray!

*Heavenly Father, please help me
not to get bogged down with the
stuff of my everyday life. Help me
to live as someone whose future
is safe with Jesus in heaven! Help
me never to forget this fact!*

Sort **sin** out!

**Colossians
3 v 5-11**

WEIRD WORDS

Earthly nature
Old sinful ways

**Immorality /
Impurity**
Sin

Lust
Wrong sexual desire

Idolatry
Worshipping things
other than God

Wrath of God
God's anger

Malice
Wanting to harm
someone

Slander
Lies about someone

**Renewed in
knowledge**
Learning from Jesus

Yesterday Paul told us to focus on heaven and not get bogged down with earthly stuff.

If we're going to put God first and concentrate on Him, we need to get rid of the bad things that get in our way.

Read Colossians 3 v 5-9

God hates sin. He can't stand it. That's why He will punish people who continue to sin instead of living for Him (v6).

Christians have turned away from doing wrong and have turned to God. So they need to try and keep sin out of their lives.

Unjumble these anagrams of some of the sins Paul mentions.

L_____   G_____
  TULS   REDGE

A_____   L_____
  RANGE   GINLY

S_____
  XESLAU

I_____
  MIMROTILYA

Think!

Read the verses again.
Which of these things do YOU struggle with?

_____

_____

_____

_____

Action prayer!

On scrap paper, write down ways of avoiding doing these wrong things. Go on...
Now ask God to help you. Do this every day if you can.

Now read verses 9-11

What does that mean?!

Verse 9

Christians have turned away from their old sinful ways.

Verse 10

They are being changed to follow Jesus. Through His Holy Spirit, He's in their lives, helping them to live for Him!

Verse 11

The truths in these verses are true for all Christians, no matter who they are or where they come from!

Christian clothes line

Tracksuit and trainers?

Or string vest and sandals?

Does it matter what you wear?

Paul says that it does!

WEIRD WORDS

Holy
Set apart to serve God

Compassion
Loving kindness

Humility
Putting other people first

Grievance
Complaint

Virtues
Good qualities

In the frame on the right, draw what you think a Christian should wear!

Okay, so Paul doesn't tell us where we should shop! But Paul does tell us what God's chosen people (Christians) should **clothe** themselves in. He means the **good qualities** Christians should show in their lives.

Read Colossians 3 v 12-14

Fill in the vowels (AEIOU) to show what these seven top qualities are.

C__MP__SS__ __N

K__NDN__SS

H__M__L__TY

G__NTL__N__SS

P__T__ __NC__

F__RG__V__N__SS

L__V__

And which is the most important? (v14)

In the 3 boxes, write the names of 3 people you know (both young and old). Now write how you can show one of these qualities in your friendship with them.

| Who: _____ |
| How: _____ |
| _____ |

| Who: _____ |
| How: _____ |
| _____ |

| Who: _____ |
| How: _____ |
| _____ |

Why should Christians show these qualities? Because God loves them (v12) and has forgiven them for all the wrong stuff they've done (v13).

Pray!

Ask God to help you show these seven good qualities. Especially the three things you've written down today.

All for Jesus

**Colossians
3 v 15-17**

*Christians come
in all shapes and
sizes.*

*But it doesn't
matter what
another believer
is like, or if they
annoy us.*

*Paul tells us
we've got to get
along with them
anyway.*

WEIRD WORDS

**Dwell among
you richly**
Live in you and
change your life

Admonish
Warn

Psalms
Songs praising God

*By the way, all of today's missing
words come from the centre of
the page.*

Read Colossians 3 v 15

**Christians are all members
of one b_____**

We're all in the same family, with
Jesus as the Head of it!

**Do you treat other Christians
as your brothers and sisters?**

**Christians must let
the p_____ of
C_____ rule in
their hearts**

Jesus is in charge of Christians'
lives. He has forgiven their sins
and brought peace into their
lives. So He expects them to act in
peace and kindness towards other
believers.

**Do you treat other Christians in a
way that would please Jesus?**

Read verse 16

**Let the m_____ of Christ
dwell among you...**

The brilliant message of Jesus and
what He's done should be at the
centre of our lives together. Let's
see how...

badger body care Christ hymns hers Lord Luton Jesus message mice
palms psalms peace peach thanks tanks teach tickle Welsh wisdom

**... as you t_____
each other with all
w_____, singing
p_____,
h_____ and songs from
the Spirit to God with
gratitude in your hearts.**

The message of Jesus is at the
centre of Christians' lives. So they
should be using God's word to
teach, warn, and help each other
live for Him. Worshipping God
together.

**How can you do this with
other believers?**

Read verse 17

**Everything you do and say
should be done in the name
of the L_____ J_____,
giving t_____ to God
the Father.**

Pray!

Ask God to help you live your life
for Jesus. Now spend five minutes
thanking God for some of the
things He's done in your life.

Master plan

Today, Paul gives us great advice for three different types of relationships:

Husbands and wives, children and parents, workers and bosses.

WEIRD WORDS

Fitting in the Lord
The right way to live for God

Embitter
Cause them to be bitter

Sincerity of heart
Really meaning it

Reverence
Respect

1. Husbands and wives
Read Colossians 3 v 18-19

> "Wives, s__bm__t to your husbands. Husbands, l__v__ your wives."

A Christian wife should honour her husband as head of the family. Just as all Christians submit to Jesus Christ as the Head of the Christian family. But a husband shouldn't take advantage. He should show love to his wife and never treat her badly.

2. Children and parents
Read verses 20-21

> "Children, __b__y your p__r__nts."

Just like the fifth commandment says, we should honour and obey our parents. Write down ways you can do this.

_____

_____

_____

Do it, it pleases God! (v20)

3. Workers and bosses
Read Colossians 3 v 22 – 4 v 1

In Bible times, rich people had slaves serving them in their homes. But these tips are relevant to all kinds of work. That means at school too!

> "O__e__ your masters in __v__ryth__ng" (v22)

Not so you look good and impressive, but out of love and respect for God.

> "Whatever you do, work at it with all your h__ __rt" (v23)

> "It is _____ you are serving" (v24)

Work hard as if you're working for Jesus — because you are! He rewards those who serve Him. But God punishes those who choose not to serve Him (v25).

Pray!

Ask God to help you obey your parents and work hard with all your heart. Ask Him to help you do it to please Him and serve Him.

Tip top trio of top tips

Colossians
4 v 2-6

Do you find it hard to pray?

Find it difficult talking to your non-Christian friends?

Then Paul has some top tips for you...

Top Tip 1:
Be devoted to prayer
Read Colossians 4 v 2

Christians need to be watchful, serving God, ready for when Jesus comes again. And they need to be **thankful** for what God has done for them.

Write down stuff to thank God for.

_____

_____

_____

_____

_____

Top Tip 2:
Pray for other Christians
Read verses 3-4

We need to pray for people who tell others about Jesus. We must ask God to open doors for them to share the message of Jesus.

Who could you pray for?

_____

_____

_____

Top Tip 3:
Take your chances
Read verses 5-6

Be wise — don't miss opportunities for chatting to friends about God. Our conversation should be full of grace and salt! That means it should be about **Jesus**. And it should be tasty like salt — pleasant and interesting!

Action!
"Know how to answer everyone." (v6)

We need to be prepared for the tricky questions people fire at us. That means knowing more of the Bible.

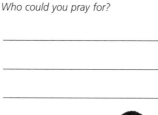

Pray!

Spend time talking to God about the things and the people you've written down.

For a free fact sheet on *HOW TO TELL PEOPLE ABOUT JESUS*, email discover@thegoodbook.co.uk or check out www.thegoodbook.co.uk/contact-us to find our UK mailing address.

Final **farewell**

We're at the
end of Paul's
letter to the
Christians in
Colossae.

We've learned
loads about
living for God.
Maybe you'd
like to flick
back through
Colossians,
noting down
great things
you've learned.

WEIRD WORDS

**Faithful
minister**
He serves God,
telling people about
Jesus

Will of God
What God wants

Fully assured
Confident that
they've had their
sins forgiven

Read Colossians 4 v 7-18

*Paul mentions loads of his Christians
friends. Unjumble the names of
the two who delivered Paul's letter
(v7-9).*

T_____
C U S I T C H Y

O_____
I O U M E S S N

And the six people who sent
greetings to the Colossians.

A_____
R I C H S T A R U S A

M_____
K R A M

J_____
S T U S U J

E_____
P A P E R S H A

L_____
K U L E

D_____
E D A M S

Let's look at two of them —
Tychicus and Epaphras.

Read verses 7-8 again

Tychicus was going to encourage
the Colossian Christians, telling
them how Paul and the other
Christians were getting along.

Action!

Which Christian friends can you
encourage this week?

_____

_____

_____

How will you do it?

_____

_____

_____

_____

Will you actually do it?

Read verse 12 again

Epaphras was always wrestling
in prayer for the Colossians. He
prayed that they would stand firm,
as mature Christians, convinced of
what they believe.

Action!

Write down the names of other
Christians you know.

_____

_____

_____

Will you pray Epaphras' prayer for
them?

DISCOVER
COLLECTION

ISSUE 5

DISCOVER ISSUE 5

Watch God bust the Israelites out of Egypt in spectacular style in Exodus. Read Acts and join Paul as he tells people about Jesus, whatever the co And let John introduce you to Jesus the light of the world!

COLLECT 12 THE SET

COLLECT ALL 12 ISSUES TO COMPLETE THE DISCOVER COLLECTION

Don't forget to order the next issue of Discover. Or even better, grab a one-year subscription to make sure Discover lands in your hands as soon as it's out. Packed full of puzzles, prayers and pondering points.